T0355938

Praise for *Joy Through the Journey*

"Very few people I meet put off an immediate impression of increase like Amberly Lago. She gets you in the mindset of expansion and increase. Her stories are transformational and her method is proven. I can't wait to see how many people she impacts with this book and message."

—**Coach Micheal Burt,**
22-time author of books including
Wall Street Journal bestseller, *Flip the Switch*

"In Joy Through the Journey, *Amberly Lago masterfully blends personal anecdotes with actionable strategies to help readers navigate their darkest moments. This book is a powerful guide to rediscovering joy and living with renewed gratitude. Amberly's insights will inspire you to embrace life's journey with resilience and hope."*

—**Leah Amico,**
three-time Olympic Gold medalist and speaker

*"*Joy Through the Journey *by Amberly Lago is a powerful and transformative guide for anyone seeking to reclaim their joy and live authentically. This book will ignite the reader's inner fire, encouraging them to embrace their imperfections and align with their true self. An inspiring and life-changing read!"*

—**Rudi Riekstins,**
leadership visionary, business mentor
and coach, and speaker

"*Whether attending her live event, joining her Mastermind, or within the pages of this brand-new book, spending time with Amberly Lago is always an inspiring and uplifting experience. She is the real deal! I love this new book and how it guides me to tap into indeed more joy in the journey. What a gift this book is and one that I'll return to again and again!*"

—Tiffany Peterson,
TEDx speaker, top 1% podcast host,
and coach

"*This book is an unparalleled guide to finding joy even in the midst of sorrow and pain. Amberly reminds us that no one is exempt from life's challenges—whether it's addiction, abuse, depression, or loss—but we all have access to the profound well of gratitude within us. Through her deeply personal experiences, she not only shares her journey to accessing joy but also provides practical steps to awaken authentic joy in your life, no matter the circumstances. Her raw, real, and honest voice transforms challenges into opportunities to draw gratitude and joy closer. If you're navigating a difficult season or climbing to the next level, this book is an essential companion.*"

—Brooke Hemingway,
speaker, high-performance coach,
and creator of Align for Success

JOY
THROUGH
THE
Journey

FOREWORD BY **JON GORDON**
BESTSELLING AUTHOR OF *THE ENERGY BUS*

AMBERLY LAGO

JOY

THROUGH
THE
Journey

Shift YOUR MINDSET,
Embrace THE PRESENT MOMENT,
AND *Cultivate Resilience*
THROUGH LIFE'S UPS AND DOWNS

WILEY

Published by John Wiley & Sons, Inc., Hoboken, New Jersey.
Published simultaneously in Canada.

For general information on our other products and services or for technical support, please contact our Customer Care Department within the United States at (800) 762-2974, outside the United States at (317) 572-3993 or fax (317) 572-4002.

Wiley also publishes its books in a variety of electronic formats. Some content that appears in print may not be available in electronic formats. For more information about Wiley products, visit our web site at www.wiley.com.

Library of Congress Cataloging-in-Publication Data Is Available:

ISBN 9781394265541 (cloth)
ISBN 9781394265558 (ePub)
ISBN 9781394265565 (ePDF)

Cover Design: Wiley
Author Photo: © Johnny Lavallee

SKY10096486_012125

For my husband, Johnny, who holds my hand and has my heart.
For my daughters, Savanna and Ruby Lee, my biggest inspirations.

Contents

Foreword

Jon Gordon

I am an encourager and I often find other voices of encouragement who are making a big difference in this world. When I meet these encouragers, I love supporting and sharing their work with others.

In this spirit I'm excited and honored to write the foreword to this book, written by my inspirational and encouraging friend Amberly Lago.

You might know Amberly from her appearances on NBC's *Today Show* or one of her numerous features in magazines like *Shape*, *Fit Pregnancy*, or *Health and Disability Magazine*. Perhaps you've been inspired by her TEDx Talk or one of her other excellent speaking engagements, subscribed to her podcast, followed her on social media, or read her first book, *True Grit and Grace*. Amberly is truly a person of fortitude, grit, and determination.

No one survives what she has—a near-death motorcycle accident, being told she had a 1% chance of saving her leg from amputation, 34 surgeries in a span of just a few years, and narrowly avoiding being in a wheelchair for the rest of her life—without Amberly's particular brand of fortitude. *True Grit and Grace* tells that story and more. No spoilers here, but suffice it to say that relearning how to walk—and eventually, run—was not the first mountain Amberly had to summit in her life.

Amberly invited my wife, Kathryn, and me to appear on her podcast, *The Amberly Lago Show: Stories of True Grit and Grace*. The experience was so good that I asked her to be a guest on my podcast in the following year. In true Amberly fashion, she showed up focused and ready to share the compelling story of her motorcycle accident. She spoke passionately about how she'd learned through her painful recovery process to turn tragedy into triumph and live a life of grit and grace.

After we finished recording her episode, I remember being struck by how joyfully she spoke—both on the podcast and off. It gave me an idea. "Amberly," I said, "I am really good at book titles, and your next book should be titled *Joy Through the Journey*."

It was so clear to me. The way Amberly continually works to be positive and cultivate joy for herself and those around her, regardless of circumstances, is simply *inspiring*. Told through the lens of her unique experience, a book about joy had the potential to help so many others live with more joy.

Today, having read *Joy Through the Journey*, I can attest not only to the potential of her message but also to its power.

In this book, Amberly mines her experiences to share the techniques and tips she uses to redirect her focus away from pain and toward joy. Using storytelling and strategies, she provides resources and guidance for readers who want more positivity and resilience in their lives. For the first time, Amberly also delves deep into her journey with addiction, sobriety, and living with complex regional pain syndrome. At times hilarious, raw, and vulnerable, her candid message will inspire you to cultivate joy in your own life.

Most of us need to learn how to choose joy and bring joy into our life, and that's why I believe this book is going to speak to you and all who read it.

Amberly had to work at being joyful, and due to this process she has become a great teacher, and we, her readers, are the beneficiary of the lessons she has learned and the joy she shares.

That's the true power of *Joy Through the Journey*. With every sentence, Amberly assures us we can keep going, joyfully, and become better versions of ourselves.

Because we are better together.

—Jon Gordon,
17-time best-selling author of *The Energy Bus*
and *The Power of Positive Leadership*

Introduction
Falling off the Wagon

Not long ago, when I'd just begun writing this book, something horribly embarrassing happened to me. It was the kind of thing that makes a person want to crawl under the covers and never come out.

Two separate times, I'd gotten an infection that put me in urgent care. The second time, the doctor laid out my choices: I could be admitted to the hospital for IV antibiotics or try a different prescription I took on my own.

She did *not* recommend the second option.

"I'll take the prescription," I said.

"The side effects are really bad," she countered. "You could rupture a tendon."

I assured her I would be fine. *I have grit*, I thought. *I know how to push through physical pain and discomfort.* After all, I live every day with a nerve disease that's ranked highest on the pain scale—I get through days when it feels like there's an ice pick jabbing me in the foot and fire ants covering my feet all the time. I knew I could just keep going.

The doctor didn't look happy, but I smiled and did what I could do to comfort her and set her mind at ease. "I have a big day ahead," I said. "This is going to work."

Boy, was I wrong.

I got my meds from the pharmacy and swallowed them on an empty stomach. I'd skipped my morning workout to go to urgent care; I'd skipped my morning ritual of reading, writing, and asking God to walk with me through the day. And there was no time for food. I had three virtual events to deliver a keynote to, a client, and I was going live on Instagram to help another client promote her new book.

I was off to the races.

Thankfully, adrenaline kicked in and my pain seemed to disappear for a bit. I gave those three keynotes every last bit of my energy. *One more thing to do*, I told myself, *and then I can come up for air*. I'd eat something, maybe even rest. My mind agreed with the grit in my work ethic, pushing right along with me. My body decided, *nah*. It couldn't push anymore.

But I had no time for giving myself grace. I logged on for the live Instagram event, where thousands of people were waiting.

And crashed.

It was almost like I was blacked out but still conscious enough to know everything was going horribly wrong. *Come on, brain!* I told myself. *WORK!* But my words weren't even coming out right. I cut the event short and passed out. I didn't even make it to the bed—just collapsed right there on the sofa and slept until morning.

As horrible as that might sound, it was far worse when I woke up to dozens of concerned messages from clients and friends. The particulars varied, but the main concern was pretty consistent: they could all tell something was off. I hadn't been myself. One person even thought I'd fallen off the wagon after years of hard-won sobriety.

Well, I hadn't. I was still sober as they day was long. But what had happened seemed far more damaging. I felt like I'd fallen off the wagon emotionally, physically, and spiritually.

I was beat.

I was embarrassed.

I was scared.

Going Bankrupt

The day of that fateful Instagram Live, I reminded myself, I *had* just gotten out of urgent care. But long before that I'd begun to let my workouts slip so I could take an extra coaching call if one of my clients had an "emergency." I'd started skipping the 12-step meetings that fueled me spiritually so I could help promote someone else's podcast. I'd made a practice of skipping meals so I could stay on Zoom just a little longer. Forget "falling off the wagon." I'd become mentally, physically, and spiritually *bankrupt*.

Something had to change.

After apologizing for my actions and behavior on that Instagram Live, I took a good hard look at the part I'd played in that potentially career-decimating outcome. Of course there had been warning signs, like when I missed a recent appointment for the first time in 20 years because I was feeling sick enough to lie down in the middle of the day—and had slept right through my alarm. At the time, it worried my client because it was so out of character for me.

Truth was, it had worried me, too. So did the fact that I'd been feeling anxious enough to tell my sponsor, "I feel my heart beating all the time—almost like palpitations—kind of the way I feel sometimes before I get onstage." The difference was, when I got onstage, adrenaline always kicked in when I stepped into the spotlight and everything felt awesome. But these anxious palpitations happened nonstop from the moment I woke up through trying to fall asleep at night.

"You're not taking care of yourself," my sponsor had responded.

"I know," I told her. Not for the first time, I was funneling all my energy into taking care of other people. I knew it. But I still couldn't quite shift gears enough to take care of me.

I thought back to that Instagram Live. When I got on that interview and wasn't myself, I thought, *What am I doing? I'm going to destroy everything I have worked so hard to build if I keep pushing this hard.* I remembered what my friend Jessie told me once, years before, when she'd seen me doing the same thing. "Amberly," she'd said, "your impact is only as strong as you are healthy."

It hit me hard when she said it—hard enough to stick. So why had I continued to push so hard? Why had I chosen to grit it out instead of giving myself grace? Why did I always seem to put others' needs before mine to the point of nearly destroying everything I've worked for years, *decades*, to achieve? Yes, I love helping others.

But why wasn't I helping myself?

Limiting Beliefs: The Little Girl That I Was

It took some soul-searching, but I had my answer. When it came right down to it, I didn't feel like I deserved help. And let me tell you, that limiting belief was deep-seated. I had long ago convinced myself that my needs were secondary (if they even ever rose as high as second on my list of important things). And in supporting others, I had lost sight of my own self.

But sometimes we have to get to such a low place—and get real humble—so we can remember what's really important. For me, in that moment, it took looking at why I had those feelings of unworthiness—why I felt everyone else deserved to feel safe, taken care of, and worthy of grace and compassion—in the first place.

Eventually I realized that those feelings, and the certainty they'd grown into, came from a moment when I was a little girl. If you've read my first book, *True Grit and Grace*, you know a little of my background. You know that my stepdad hurt me for years, and that when I gathered enough courage to tell my real dad about the sexual abuse I was routinely subjected to, Dad did nothing to stop it. He had his reasons, and when I was an adult he explained them to me. But when I held that experience up to the light, I understood how it made me feel like he didn't protect me *because I didn't deserve protection.*

That little girl, who felt like she wasn't worth protecting or loving or being taken care of, was still with me as an adult. In other words, my spectacular Instagram fail had begun long, long before I started feeling sick or even missing appointments. It started that day at my Dad's house.

I couldn't have known that or seen this particular public consequence coming. But, as I said, all this unfolded while I was in the process of *writing a book about joy.* The irony didn't escape me. *If I'm going to write a book on joy*, I thought, *well, my gosh—I better spark some.*

Like so many things in life, I couldn't change what had happened. I couldn't change that I'd gotten caught up in the momentum of my career and, as a result, wound up stuck in my little office for 12 or 14 hours a day, with no sun, no breaks, no exercise, doing back-to-back Zoom calls. What kind of life is that?

I wasn't doing it anymore.

Instead, I recommitted to practices that would help me come into realignment with my own well-being.

Reflect and Recommit

Without your health, you lose your relationships, business, reputation, and even your mind. Even worse, you could lose your life. It's not like I didn't know all that, and you would think that going septic once after a kidney infection and winding up in the intensive care unit—and hearing a doctor tell me that if I'd waited one more day to come in, I would be dead—would have scared me enough that I would've paid attention to the alarms going off in my body. But I've always been good at grit, to a detriment. It was only when I realized I couldn't make an impact and help others if I was unhealthy that really got me.

"You know what, Amberly?" my sponsor said. "I want you to do something every day that's going to take care of you the way you take care of other people. I want you to do something to take care of yourself."

Of course, she was right. I could—and needed to—tell that little girl in me that I am worthy of being taken care of and doing things that bring me joy.

Right out of the gate, I also had to let go of the shame I felt over making a fool of myself in front of thousands of people. So I shined a light on it. I made apologies, faced every text from concerned friends. *Heck*, I thought, *I'm glad they cared enough to reach out*. I returned phone calls and assured everyone that I was going to take care of myself—and this time, I meant it.

I decided I would even do an episode on my show, *The Amberly Lago Show*, and share all the lessons I had learned and what I was doing to improve. Sure, I did this to help listeners, but I also did it to hold myself accountable.

I also looked at the part I'd played that day of the Instagram Live to see what I could change. I couldn't *unmake* a fool of myself, but I could show up differently from that point on.

If you're reading this and have experienced this kind of embarrassment from your own hand (the worst kind, isn't it?), get radically honest with yourself. Take a good hard look at what isn't working. Ask yourself, "How's that working for ya?" and accept the fact that everything you do is either helping you or hurting you. It's either moving you closer to your goal—moving the needle on your business *and* your health—or it's hurting you. Get objective with you and call it like it is.

Me, I wasn't doing myself any favors by skipping all the practices I'd cultivated to help me live a full, joy-filled life. So I recommitted to reading out of my daily reflection books, writing in my journal, and doing what Mel Robbins calls *brain dumping*, so I could get all the negative feelings out of my head and tame that inner critic. When you read, you learn about the world and others, but when you *write*, you learn about yourself.

I also made another call to my sponsor, who always makes me feel better. "We can do good on the outside if we're working on our insides," she reminded me. In other words, when we focus on improving our inner selves—our mindset, emotions, and values—we are better equipped to do good in the world and positively affect those around us. Whether it's a sponsor, a mentor, a good friend who'll risk calling you out, or a therapist, have people you can confide in. For the record, I have them all. She'd also asked me to write down the things I did each day to take care of me, and having the accountability helped. I started making it a point to check in with someone, usually a sober sister, every day.

Mental practices, *check*.

Within a week, I had my first day without feeling like my heart wasn't beating out of my chest. I still determined to address what was going on with me physically—I wanted to know why my body was trying to tell me something was wrong. I saw a functional doctor and had bloodwork done.

Listen, people—numbers don't lie. When I got the results back, so many things were off. They explained why I'd been feeling anxious to the point that my hair was falling out. The doctor recommended supplements, drinking more water, sleeping more, and keeping my workouts in check. I made those things part of my new business strategy, and I'm already seeing more consistency in my workouts and I'm more intentional about how I move my body.

Holistically addressing my health also helped me set healthy boundaries around my time. I started saying no to things that would drain me—Zoom meetings, podcast guesting invitations, and even three different event planners who approached me about potential speaking gigs. I'd finally recognized how important it is to take time for my mental and physical health, and I was committed to protecting them. If I didn't, everything would come crashing down around me. After all, I was living proof of that.

But I still wasn't done overhauling—I needed to address my spiritual health.

I got down on my knees and prayed, and if I couldn't go to church, I listened to my pastor online. I started my day with the gratitude practice I'd honed after a life-altering motorcycle accident—and the 34 surgeries that followed—almost took my leg and my life. I shared my gratitude with a special group of women I affectionately refer to as my God Squad gals. Finally, I decided to go to more 12-step recovery program meetings. I even promised my sponsor I would text her after each one.

All these things together helped me then and continue helping me today. I just needed to take a pause and figure out they were needed.

I think one of the most important things we can do in our lives is to pause. To breathe, take a step back, be still, and quiet our minds. When we pause, we put ourselves in a place to reflect and gain perspective. Sometimes that pause is necessary in a heated moment, so we can consider our response. Sometimes we need to pause when we reach a crossroads in life so we can consider our next steps—what we want most and how to get there. Other times, like it was for me, we need to pause after a busy period to rest, relax, and reflect.

About This Book

Truth be told, I'd started feeling sick the week before Instagram, but I kept pushing through, pushing through, pushing through. By the next week, I was a mess—an absolute mess. But this is a book about finding joy—so what does this experience have to do with the price of eggs in China? Simply this: in order to find joy and keep finding it, we have to acknowledge some truths about the ups and downs of growth and healing.

Lots of people think growing and healing are linear. Nope. That couldn't be farther from the truth. They think, *Oh, once I've found joy I'll always be joyful.* No—it gets knocked right out of you. Same goes for resilience and confidence. We bounce forward, we slip up. We build momentum, then we lag. Sometimes you fall down and you have to get back up and *start over completely.*

Similarly, too many people seem to believe that joy and pain are either/or—if you're in the throes of one of them, you can't have the other. Well, that's just plain wrong. But I can attest that it feels very, very true sometimes. There have been times in my life when things got pretty dark. There was a time when I didn't think joy would ever be a part of my life. But I realized that joy comes from deep within us. It's up to us to do the things that deepen our joy.

Repeat after me: we will never cross a boundary and find ourselves in a place where good is perpetual and setbacks don't exist. But with the right tools, we can get through the tough times— and find joy in the process.

That's what this book is for. I want you to have the tools to rebound from life's obstacles. Because believe me, they're coming. I'm going to tell you all about some of the worst ones I've experienced—from being abused as a child, to surviving the motorcycle accident that almost took my leg, to enduring the 34 surgeries that saved it, to asking my doctor for an amputation, to using alcohol as medicine when the pain felt like more than I could take. Pain has been one of my closest companions since I was a kid, but none of it was wasted. It prepared me for the next thing, and the next, and the next.

And it did not end my joy forever—it helped me fight harder to spark it and keep it.

Key Takeaway

You deserve to have your needs met. You are *worth* having your needs met. Achieving mental and physical well-being ignites the spark of joy within, illuminating the path to a fulfilling life. When we prioritize self-care, we fuel our inner light, radiate joy and vitality, brighten our days, and inspire others.

1

The Moment I Discovered Joy

I think my mom put me in dance when I was a kid because it was the girly thing to do and I was always such a tomboy. I had my curls cropped short like Shirley Temple's, and like her, whenever I danced I came alive. In fact, I was fearless about it. When I danced, it wasn't about me. It was about all the people watching, about how I saw them smiling. Their faces lit up.

That's where the joy was.

Well, one night, everyone in my town was celebrating our high school football team's recent win. Football is big in Texas, and it seemed like the whole town had squeezed into that little restaurant. Every table was filled and it was standing room only. There were parents, members of the marching band still in uniform, you name it. The way I remember, they were all clapping their hands along with the jukebox. I was young enough

1

that I don't really remember how I got there or how I got home, but I remember the smiles and the music and the smell of French fries. I started dancing, and before long someone picked me up and put me on a tabletop.

You better believe I kept on dancing.

It felt like freedom. It's the same kind of feeling I get now when I'm onstage as a speaker—an intense, giddy wave of *this is where I'm meant to be*. You'd think neither of those places—a tabletop in a burger joint and a stage in front of thousands of people—would ever feel safe, but safe is exactly what I felt. It was, in a single word, like *home*.

That night, looking at all the faces around me, peace, contentment, and pure satisfaction washed over me. I didn't know the word *joy* then, let alone what it meant, but I experienced it all the same. I knew I wanted it again. I took to dancing anywhere and everywhere the opportunity presented itself. We'd meet someone in the aisles of the supermarket or on the sidewalk, and I'd give 'em a little tap dance when they asked. When I wasn't actually dancing, I was looking forward to it. Dance always gave me that—the next burst of joy, the next smile my little feet coaxed out of someone in my life. Once I had dance, I always had something to look forward to.

I couldn't have known that first night, up there on that tabletop, that years later I would stare into the abyss of my full-blown addiction to alcohol, thinking one horrible thought.

How did a good girl like you end up like this?

Before I Knew It

Heading west about 25 miles an hour on my Harley along Ventura Boulevard in Woodland Hills, I stopped at a red light and was first at the line, with only a couple of cars behind me. When the light turned green, I had the right lane to myself and was going about 20 miles an hour when I noticed that, ahead of me about 40 yards, an SUV was stopped at the end of a car dealership's driveway, waiting to turn into traffic. Its driver, a middle-aged man, and I exchanged eye contact, so I felt assured of my safety knowing he saw me. I assumed he planned to do what he was legally and logically supposed to do: wait for me, and the cars behind me, to pass before pulling out.

But that's not what happened.

He punched the gas just as I reached the driveway. I saw him in my peripheral vision, and in a millisecond understood what was going on and recognized there was absolutely nothing I could do—no evasive action possible—to avoid being rammed by this big Ford Flex. If I didn't know better, I'd say he was actually trying to hit me. Anyway, it was a difference without distinction.

The noise of the impact sticks in my memory as something between a bomb and a bullet, but it's the pain that's most stuck with me because—well, it's still with me.

Having given birth twice, I can best describe the immediate, searing, piercing agony as what you imagine real torture victims endure at the hands of professional sadists—though I imagine knowing someone is intentionally trying to inflict maximum pain on you adds a whole new level of suffering. This was enough.

A witness later told me I looked as if I'd been catapulted into the air. I only remember sliding down Ventura Boulevard on the asphalt as if I were on a grinding stone, thinking, *Please don't let another car hit me*. I heard no brakes screeching, no bystanders scream, no horns honking—all of which, I later learned, actually had filled the air.

When I at last came to a stop I instinctively tucked into a fetal position to protect myself from being hit again. No one rushed to me. I lie there alone and noticed people walking slowly, apprehensively, no doubt wondering whether they should venture out into this mess. And then I glanced at my leg and realized their hesitancy, not to mention their faces frozen in horror, had to do with how bad off I looked.

Every beat of my heart issued a geyser of blood from what was a ruptured femoral artery in the middle of tissue damage that looked like a mangled mess of tissue. I grabbed for what was left of my leg and tried to keep the pieces from falling off and the blood from gushing. As much as it hurt, and as horrifying as it was, I found myself looking at it as if from afar, trying to decide how to describe it while I was looking at it. My right foot, for example, attached only by skin and my torn black leggings, dangled from the shin like a broken flowerhead.

Somewhere between five seconds and five minutes passed before I yelled out, "F---! Someone call 9-1-1!" and then, "And call my husband!" followed by his cell phone number. My proper Methodist mother came to mind and I suddenly felt guilty for cussing, which led me to think about my job. *Oh, I guess I'm going to have to train my clients on crutches for a while*, which was a truly insane thought. Crutches? Anyone could see that I'd be lucky to keep my leg. And luckier still to survive. Yet I wasn't done with the insanity. I actually wondered whether Johnny would be pissed that a pulled pork sandwich had messed up his new backpack—his new backpack that, as I realized later, had actually saved my life because it was on my back that I'd slid after being hit. Without it, the grinding on the asphalt for that long a distance would've shredded my jacket and probably my skin and tissue right down to the spine. It's not for nothing that serious cycle riders wear outfits of leather.

I'm not sure if it was 10 seconds or 10 minutes before an honest-to-goodness good Samaritan came over to me, slipped off his belt, and fashioned it into a tourniquet around my leg. That simple act stopped the artery from spurting, and I'm not sure I even thanked him. He was like the Lone Ranger—just did his thing and left without knowing that, to this day, I think of him as a guardian angel.

Soon a middle-aged lady approached me and in a calm voice identified herself as a nurse. She clasped my hands and asked me to focus on breathing normally. She did it herself as an example, breathing in through her nose, and slowly out her mouth, knowing I'd automatically emulate her. But what made a much more powerful impression on me was her touch—holding my hands. I felt so grateful for that, especially because the driver who'd hit me just stood there, about eight feet away, arms across his chest, his face void of visible emotion, no doubt upset that he wouldn't soon be wherever he was in such a hurry to get to that he couldn't wait an extra five seconds.

The front bumper of his car had been sheared off by the impact.

With.

My.

Leg.

A crowd had begun to gather. One woman wandered over for a better view and got more than she'd bargained for. Fortunately, she didn't fall over like a tree when she fainted, which might have cracked her head; she simply crumpled the way dainty ladies do in movies.

I heard sirens and wondered whether they were for me. They were. Two ambulances, a fire truck, and an LAPD cruiser pulled up at about the same time. Johnny, who'd been waiting for me at home, came in right behind them in his truck. I'd shouted out his phone number so many times, a bunch of the bystanders had called him. Not recognizing the names or numbers in his caller ID, he'd let the first several calls go to voicemail, wondering what the hell was happening, before realizing that something serious must be up. By now, the cops had shut down Ventura Boulevard. Johnny pushed through the crowd that had gathered around me.

The look on his face is etched in my memory. It was a heart-breaking mix of horror, sadness, and panic.

But at least he was looking at me. The paramedics showed no emotion, which I understood, but they wouldn't make eye contact, which I didn't understand. Or did I? Was I assuming correctly that my condition was far worse than even the excruciating pain indicated? Were they trying to avoid a human-to-human connection with someone they thought would soon be dead?

With practiced skill, the paramedics got me onto a board, immobilized my head and neck, and strapped me down. The pain was indescribable, meaning I can't possibly find the words to describe it other than to say that on a 0–10 pain scale, this was 659. I have passed a kidney stone and given birth twice, and I'd have put those at no more than an eight on the pain scale. Even if I hadn't been gritting my teeth and moaning, the paramedics would've known by the looks of things what I was enduring.

That 15-minute drive to the hospital seemed more like 15 years! When I arrived at the hospital they put me in an induced coma because they couldn't control my pain and my vital organs were shutting down. Holding my husband's hand was the last thing I remember until I woke up over a week later and learned I had a 1% chance of saving my leg.

I took that chance and Dr. Wiss performed 34 surgeries to save it. I go into more detail about the months I was in the hospital in my first book, but it was brutal, humbling to have to use a bedpan, and also life-changing to say the least.

The period following my motorcycle accident in 2010 was one of pain, striving to heal, and personal growth, but it also ushered in the life and career I have now, making it an integral part of the life I love. But I spent a lot of time in the weeds of denial. I didn't want to accept the way I looked. I didn't want to accept my diagnoses, the medications I was supposed to take to treat my injuries, or the way I felt. I wanted to mute all that—and I wanted a way out of the chronic, searing pain I felt after I was diagnosed with complex regional pain syndrome (CRPS)—otherwise known as the "suicide disease."

In the face of all that denial and pain, and trying every kind of treatment under the sun to cure this pain, nothing was working and my addiction came on little by little.

I remember having a glass of wine and thinking, *Gosh, this really helps the pain.* So when I hurt, I'd knock back a glass. I knew it wasn't the healthiest thing to do. But still I thought, *If this is what I have to do to get through each day of pain, I guess I'll have a glass of wine every day.*

Well, one glass worked a little. Then it was two glasses, because two worked a little better. Before I knew it, I was drinking a bottle. The road between a bottle of wine and *Well, wine is great, but I bet if I drank vodka, that would kick the pain even faster* was short. Soon I got to the point that I was having vodka in my regular drinks—a lot of vodka—a lot of the time.

And then I was drinking it straight from the bottle.

I was hiding it.

See, I wasn't going out to bars. I wasn't partying. On, no—I was simply kicking back a glass of wine or a shot of vodka whenever I could, just to numb out the pain that felt like my foot was being held in a vice grip that just kept getting tighter. And it wasn't just the physical pain; it was emotional, too. On the outside, I was trying to pretend like everything was okay. I wanted everyone to think I was pulled together under the surface. But of course, I wasn't. I was dying inside. What I was feeling did not match the way I appeared.

Before I realized what had happened, the drinking had become a cycle I couldn't break. I was completely out of alignment with who I was. I wasn't being honest with myself, God, or anybody else. Including my husband, Johnny—a police officer.

Let me tell you—it takes *skill* to hide that kind of drinking from a cop. Especially as it continued to get worse and worse.

The Cure, or the Cause?

The whole time I was in addiction, the alcohol was slowly crushing my spirit. My confidence had disintegrated completely, and I stopped trusting myself. If you've read my first book, you know how much that self-reliance meant to me. (I'll talk about that more in later chapters, too.) I built my entire life on trusting myself. If that was gone, who or what was left for me to trust?

I'd become hopeless. My thoughts settled into a horrific, abusive loop.

See, all my life I had been so determined. When I set my mind to something, I achieved it. No questions asked. But this addiction—it had really licked me. I would tell myself, *I'm going to manage better next time, but I might as well just get drunk now.*

My brain raced uncontrollably, always with a terrible sense of impending doom.

It got to where I could eat very, very little.

Sometimes I could eat nothing at all.

One of the worst moments came after I went to the doctor for a checkup. I did the requisite bloodwork. Normally, a nurse followed up with the results. But this time, the doctor called me himself.

"Amberly," he said, "do you drink?"

"Occasionally," I said.

"Well, your liver enzymes are elevated 300 times the amount they should be."

He was trying to be so nice about it, but he and I both knew numbers didn't lie. I might've thought I was controlling my addiction, but in that moment I was forced to admit my control was slipping. For someone like me, who prided herself on having a near unlimited capacity to overcome obstacles, it was devastating. I was cornered. I was overwhelmed. I couldn't do anything about it. The loneliness, the despair, the self-pity . . . I had really, truly met my match.

Alcohol had become my master.

At some point, I began thinking of a guy I'd dated before I met Johnny. Like me, he was into fitness—Muay Thai kickboxing—and I originally knew him from work. When we started dating, we never drank together.

And then we went to Vegas.

I took him to see a fight, and it was the first time we ever had drinks together. Keep in mind, this is before my motorcycle accident, before my CRPS diagnosis. I didn't have a problem with alcohol then—and I had no idea that this guy was breaking his sobriety to have those drinks with me.

I woke up in the middle of the night to find that he'd drunk the entire minibar in our room. His personality changed—it was like he became this embodiment of evil. *What is going on?* I thought.

It wasn't until we got back home that he told me he was an alcoholic.

I went to meetings with him, but back then I just . . . did not get it at all. Why couldn't these people just have one drink and not need more?

I understand it now.

When you're in addiction, no amount of alcohol is ever enough. Your mind is obsessed. The part that craves more, more, always *more* will not stop. Fear might've sobered me up for a bit, but then came the insanity of that first drink and I would be off again.

And then there's the complete physical dependency that comes from long-term alcoholism.

One day Johnny and I met for lunch. I was still deeply in addiction, but I was trying not to drink. Johnny still didn't know exactly how much I was drinking, and I actually don't remember if I'd had any alcohol yet that day. But I do remember that I could barely eat because I had so much alcohol in my system. The idea of solid food was too much. *Soup*, I thought, trying to find something on the menu I'd be able to choke down. *I'll have a bowl of soup*.

But by that point, I had tremors if I didn't drink.

The soup arrived. Forget eating it—my hands were shaking so much I couldn't even hold the spoon.

"Why are you shaking?" Johnny asked.

My alcoholic brain raced to an explanation—aka, a cover story. "I think my blood sugar is low," I said. And in that moment, I didn't think, *Okay, I can't drink anymore.* My thought was, *Okay, don't order soup anymore. You can't hold the spoon.*

It's baffling what addiction will do to your mind. And I hated myself for not being honest with my husband.

There I was, the survivor of a near-death motorcycle accident. Of the 34 surgeries it took to save my leg.

I'd survived it all, and yet there I was. Slowly killing myself with alcohol.

Vicious Cycle

During those years, Johnny and I were having the house remodeled. One day, I walked into one of the rooms while some construction was in progress—and, yes, I'd been drinking. All the construction workers were wearing masks because they were doing work on the foundation. Clouds of thick dust were kicked up all over the place.

Our contractor looked up at me through all that dust in the air. He stopped what he was doing, grabbed me by the arm, and looked me straight in the face. "Are you okay?" he asked. "You shouldn't be in here. You need a mask."

Well, I felt seen. I felt like someone *finally saw me* through all the terrible decisions I'd been making while drinking.

I don't know when I realized it, but I *wanted* to get sober. I remember thinking, *I've got to stop.* But I couldn't. It was such a vicious cycle.

Every night before I fell asleep, I would promise myself I wasn't going to drink anymore. But the next day when I woke up, the pain would be so bad it just . . . took over. I had to drink again. The irony is that I was drinking to numb the pain, but alcohol is an inflammatory substance. It was actually making the pain worse. I would drink more, and the inflammation would violently flare up, and so I would . . . drink more. My "medicine" was the reason I kept needing so much "medicine."

One evening, my daughter Savanna had a cello concert. I thought, *Okay, I have to make it through the day without drinking so I can make it to her concert.* Thankfully, I did.

But when I got there, I saw my sister-in-law, whom I hadn't seen in a long time. I'm sure it was a shock for her. I was far enough gone in my addiction that I was puffy. I was a shell of myself. I wasn't spiritually connected; I was dead inside. And although I'd managed to not drink that day, I still had so much alcohol in my system that I'm sure I reeked of it. The next day, she called.

"I wanted to see you for coffee. Will you come?" she asked.

I said I would, even though—or maybe because—I knew she knew. The gig was up. This coffee date wasn't about her or anyone else she'd invited. It was about me.

I showed up at 7 a.m. for coffee, and the questions began almost immediately.

"Have you been drinking?" my sister-in-law asked. She was sober herself—she understood that she was taking a huge risk in calling me out.

"No," I said.

"Well, you reek of alcohol." She paused. "Amberly, are you okay? Do you have a problem with drinking?"

Suddenly everything hit home: I wasn't fooling anybody. Everyone could see that something wasn't right.

I burst into tears.

"Yeah," I said between sobs. "I need help."

That day I googled "12-step meeting" and found a meeting I could go to when Johnny was at work and my daughters were at school. Yes, I went from sneaking my drinking to sneaking my recovery at first. It was actually the scariest thing I have ever done to walk into the rooms of recovery for the first time. But there is a gift in desperation and I was determined to overcome this. I heard hope in the shares from all the other women, and not just that, they laughed and had so much joy. I kept going back. That was in 2016 and to this day I still find recovery AND joy in the rooms with all my sober sisters and brothers.

Reflection

Right about now you might be wondering, *What does any of this have to do with finding joy?*

In a word, *everything*. Finding joy is all about coaxing that spark of joy into a roaring flame, no matter how deeply it's buried in all the gunk life throws at us.

I didn't really talk about any of this when I wrote my first book. I was newly sober then and I still had a lot of shame. But now I can talk about it. That addicted person was me. That half-life being "lived" was mine.

That person suffering in silence was me, too.

I chose to talk about addiction here, right from the get-go, because I had so much shame about it and I know others do, too. So many people are suffering in silence. I want that to end. I want to break that stigma about addiction.

On the surface, I was so different from other people in my family with an addiction. I was a former fitness model, professional dancer, and athlete. And you know what? Addiction didn't care about the years I'd devoted to honing my body. Addiction didn't care how many hours of my life I'd spent perfecting muscles and movements. Addiction came for me just like it comes for anyone. It did not discriminate. It never does.

If it has come for you—if it's coming for you now—you can have freedom.

And you still have joy.

Not long after I began my sobriety, I spoke at an event. Afterwards, I went to dinner with all the other speakers. Everyone was ordering drinks but me. Fast-forward about a year, to the day I received a phone call from the person who'd been sitting next to me that night.

"Amberly," he said, "I just want you to know something. I didn't order a drink at dinner that night because I was sitting next to you and saw you order a sparkling water when everyone else was ordering alcohol. I thought I'd have a glass of water with you instead and be supportive of you by not drinking."

For the record, it doesn't bother me if someone else drinks. I just don't want to do it myself.

"I got back to my hotel that night," he continued, "and I couldn't go back up to my room because I *had* to have a drink before I did. So I sat at the bar and thought, 'I don't know if this is a problem, but surely it's not good that I *have* to have a drink before I can go upstairs.' It really made me think, and from that night on I stopped drinking. Because of you, I've been sober for a year."

I'd had no idea he felt that way, of course. But I will tell you that there are so many people out there who are struggling, stuffing down their feelings, their shame, and whatever pain is driving them to drink and take the edge off of what they're feeling—physical, emotional, spiritual—by knocking one back. Alcohol seems like an escape hatch, and so many of us use it.

But it doesn't work, does it?

Yes, it numbs the pain. It also numbs everything else. You can't make meaningful connections when you're drunk. It cuts off your spiritual connection to God. It keeps you from entering your power.

But in that moment when I was able to get sober, I think God—through all the physical, emotional, mental, and other layers of pain I've experienced—enabled me to walk that path so I could come out of it. So I could stand as a witness for others who are experiencing pain, take them by the hand, and show them that there is another way.

If my life has shown me anything, it's that every single thing we go through is preparing us for the thing we're destined to do for this world. Every trauma, shame, and heartache is preparing us for the next person we need to help, and then the next, and then the next. I can't tell you how many people come to me and open up about their own abuse, their own addictions, their own scars. They tell me they've been unable to walk with dignity, but that hearing my story is giving them the confidence to go after their dreams and *keep trying*. I'm going to talk about that a lot more in the coming pages.

When I was in addiction, every day I begged for mercy from the pain. I didn't know how I could get through the excruciating pain without drinking, but I found that it's possible. God didn't waste my pain. He won't waste yours, either. You and I can serve others.

When we're in service to others, we give ourselves and them purpose.

And it increases all of our joy.

I'm sure I'll say this a lot, but nothing in my life has come easily to me—least of all the joy that I treasure so dearly. No, I haven't just "been that way" since I was a kid. After that night of dancing to the jukebox, there were plenty of times when I didn't think joy was ever going to be a part of my life.

But then I realized that joy comes from deep within us. It might feel small, or nonexistent, but even when we're in the most pain, it's still there.

Luckily for us, we can embrace that fact. Joy doesn't go out the window because we have trauma or even because we're *in* trauma. When I was eight years old, my stepdad started sexually abusing me. I focused on dancing more. It didn't stop the abuse, but it helped me find joy alongside that pain.

And it taught me there are always things we can do to spark and increase our joy.

It's simply up to us to do them.

Actionable Steps

Get help if you need it. If you're in an abusive situation or in addiction, there are resources. Call someone you trust, attend a meeting, or see a therapist or physician.

Reach out for support. Connect with a trusted friend, family member, counselor, or support group. Sharing your struggles can reduce feelings of isolation and offer a safe space to express emotions. It's important to lean on a community that can provide encouragement and understanding. Connection is the opposite of addiction.

Seek professional help. Consult with a therapist, addiction specialist, or medical professional. They can provide tailored guidance, therapy, or even medication that may be needed to address both the emotional and physical aspects of addiction and pain.

Practice mindfulness and self-care. Engage in activities like meditation. I am not great at mediation so I actually use an app that guides me and this really helps. Deep breathing exercises also help. I personally like the 4, 7, 8 technique. Breath in for 4 seconds, hold for 7 seconds, then exhale for 8 seconds. This type of breathing actually calms the nervous system. Try some gentle physical movement such as walking or stretching. These practices can help calm the mind, manage stress, and improve the overall sense of well-being, offering relief from emotional and physical pain.

Create a daily routine. Establish a structured daily routine with activities that focus on self-improvement and healing. Incorporating healthy habits, such as regular sleep, nourishing your body, and moving your body however you can, can help restore stability and reduce cravings, making it easier to stay on track.

Take it one day at a time. This enables you to focus on manageable steps toward recovery, reducing the overwhelming pressure of long-term goals and helping you stay present on your journey. This also enables you to celebrate small victories along the way, boosting confidence and creating a sense of achievement.

Key Takeaway

Shift your thinking. Embrace that joy can coexist with pain.

CHAPTER

2

The Power of Acceptance

A Path to Inner Peace and Personal Growth

Sometimes we need another person to believe in us before we can believe in ourselves.

Sometimes it takes others to love us before we can love ourselves.

Sometimes—and this is harder, isn't it?—it takes a total stranger, seeing us differently than we see ourselves, for us to look at ourselves in a different way.

In my case, the first person to love and accept my scars before I could love myself was my husband, Johnny. My doctor came next. Little by little, with every expression of acceptance and love, I began to look at myself a little differently. And then came my first trip to Miami after the accident.

Okay, I thought. *I'm going to be on the beach.*

My husband's family lives in Miami, so this wasn't our first rodeo with the palms, the sunshine, the surf. But this would be my first time to wear a bathing suit without wearing pants to cover my scars.

At first, I compromised: no pants, but a flesh-colored compression sock that would camouflage some of my scars. But then I stood on the beach watching my husband. I watched my girls, who were running around in their sarongs and bikinis, splashing in the water to get Johnny's attention. After a time he walked over to me and we sat down on the sand.

"I'm taking this off," I said, and began working the sock down my leg.

"Should you do that?" he asked. "Will the sun affect it?"

But I was realizing a hard-won truth that I'd been learning for a while: embrace the stuff and keep your chin up, because *life gets better when you decide it does.*

And I had decided.

"I'm taking it off," I said.

I did, and we walked down the beach.

From then on, I let my scars show. Taking off a sock seems like such a small thing, but baring my scars to the world felt like such a big deal. I remember getting on an elevator in our hotel a few days later. Another woman in the elevator car wouldn't stop staring at me.

"Hey," she said. "I saw you in the pool yesterday. All I kept thinking was, *Wow—this girl's an overcomer.*"

I thanked her, realizing how much I had grown to be able to be there at the pool and show my scars. It was the first time anyone had seen them and looked at me like I was an inspiration—not because of my accomplishments in dance, or because I'd been in a music video for M. C. Hammer—but simply because my scars told a story about pain and survival and, yes, overcoming.

Not long after, I did a photo shoot on the beach. I showed my scars and posted the photos on Instagram. It was the first time I'd put any pictures like that on social media. Suddenly people were reaching out.

Because of you, I have the courage to accept my scars.

I don't feel like I have to be in shame about my mastectomy scars anymore.

I don't have scars on the outside, but I've got plenty on the inside. Because of you, I feel like I can let that go and step into my power.

Denial Is Not Your Superpower

Getting to that moment on the beach—that decision to wriggle that sock down my leg, consequences be damned—was a long, long process, one I described in detail in my first book. Suffice it to say that after my motorcycle accident, I was in complete denial about everything in my life.

My diagnoses and medications.

My scars.

All of it.

I was existing out of acceptance with the way I looked, felt, and lived—especially with my addiction to alcohol. Before my motorcycle accident, I'd been a model. In the gym, my nickname was Legs. After the accident, I saw my leg and thought, *Now look at me.* I felt powerless over the way I looked. I had lost my whole identity.

So one day, after enduring 34 surgeries to save my leg, I was just . . . done. I was done with all the scars AND all the pain. I desperately wanted to save my leg, but I had come to a point where I thought life would be better if it was gone.

So I asked my doctor to amputate it.

"Why would I do that?" he asked. "Your leg is a work of art."

His words hit me hard. I began to think, *If he can look at my leg this way, maybe I can, too.*

What I couldn't have known in that moment was that being able to look at those scars and accept them would become my superpower. Being able to see my scars as victories would be *the* victory for me.

But if I'd kept living in denial, I would still be stuck.

Accepting where you are is often the thing that moves you forward. That seems backwards, but it's true. Acceptance actually feeds you into community. It will allow you to make more meaningful connections and makes it possible to surround yourself with supportive networks of friends and professionals who can offer encouragement and guidance.

Sometimes it will even lead you to a career.

Someone asked me recently how I got started as a speaker. How did I learn to share a story in a way that's impactful for others? The truth is, I didn't start out on big stages. I started out every day, in my 12-step meetings, sharing my story in that small community of people I trusted. By expressing and sharing my vulnerabilities, I slowly started to build strength. As a bonus, sharing my experience gave me the gift of perspective validation. That boost of acceptance reinforced my journey toward acceptance and personal development.

For what it's worth, I think it's important to first share your story with someone outside your circle of trusted friends and family. But hear me on this: *the work of acceptance has to come first.*

If you put the cart before the horse and share your story on social media, and haven't done the work of completely accepting your appearance and imperfect past, you'll be massacred on the internet. My first foray into TikTok got me responses like, "Don't show your leg. I was eating and almost threw up" and "My God, what is this?" If that sounds horrible, it was—but I can honestly say it didn't get to me. I had already accepted my scars, my appearance. Had I not done that work? Well, I would've been devastated and probably never posted again.

Same goes for talking about my sobriety and showing my scars. I was sober for almost five years before I did a post on social media with my five-year chip. And it took that many years of covering my scars and accepting the way I looked before I could walk down that beach in Miami and feel comfortable showing my scars to the world.

Living in acceptance isn't something we either do or don't do. It isn't like flipping a switch or stepping into a different room. Just like finding and keeping joy, it is a constant practice. And it is not always easy. There are ebbs and flows.

Life is never that you're simply . . . okay.

Listen, I've accepted my scars and everything is great. But there are still hard days, like on a recent anniversary when I wanted to be able to wear a cute pair of little pumps with a strap when I went out with my husband—which I did. And let me tell you, when I got home I sat on the bathroom floor and could barely take that shoe off. My leg was so swollen it looked like a sausage, the strap digging mercilessly into my ankle. My husband found me there, lamenting.

"Oh, look at my leg," I said.

"Yeah," he replied, "look at your leg. Isn't it a miracle?"

Yes. It is.

My whole life, I was somebody who ran from everything. I ran from pain. I ran from shame. I always say that my pain fueled me, and it's true. I think that's how I became successful in track and set a state record. I think it's how I had a successful career and built my business in the fitness industry. I think it was how I became a successful professional dancer.

And yet, I was in denial—struggling to try and control what I couldn't.

When we deny something exists, we can't change it. If we insist we're not hurting, we'll never heal. Me, I was always trying to cover up the fact that I was hurting. I was trying to cover up the fact that I felt so lonely. Nobody understood me. I was so scared and was pretending like I wasn't.

When we do that—when we're in denial—there's no opportunity to learn how to feel better. There's no opportunity for meaningful connection. We're just going about our day-to-day and dealing with our feelings. That's no way to live. Only when we tell ourselves the truth and risk seeing ourselves as we are can we begin to experience change.

I am powerless to change my scars. Powerless to go back in time and prevent the motorcycle accident that gave them to me. But my scars are all the hard things I've overcome. And they're proof of how amazing and strong the human spirit is.

They're proof that we can heal.

We heal what we reveal. When I stepped out of denial and into acceptance, I could reveal all the parts of me that needed healing. And I freed myself and my attention to focus on areas that I *could* control. That's why I say acceptance enables us to take action with grit.

And *that's* how we become powerful.

Accepting Imperfection

After my accident, I felt so imperfect, and I still do. But accepting imperfection and embracing my scars has given me the opportunity to heal in other areas of my life. It has enabled me to connect with others. It has given me purpose.

While I was working on this book, I was wrestling and horsing around with my daughter—we do that sometimes—and I fell. I hit the edge of a table, busted my nose, and gave myself two black eyes. I needed nine stitches in my forehead, and I now have a scar on my face. When it happened, all I could think was, *Great. First the scars on my leg. Now I have one on my face. Awesome.*

But let me tell you: perfect is boring. (I always say I would rather be courageous and stand out in my group than be perfect.) Even more important, when you stand in acceptance of who you are and where you are on your journey, no one can hold those "bad" things against you.

Accepting the scars on my leg taught me to live in acceptance with other parts of my life. And trust me—I needed to. Before I got sober, I'd spent plenty of time in denial about my alcoholism. If someone had asked me during that period whether I was drinking too much, or if I had a problem, I would have been humiliated. Devastated. It would've filled me with so much shame.

Shame is the lowest frequency we can feel. At that point in my life, I was already there. And you know what? It's hard to love yourself from that place of darkness. In my personal darkness—in some moments—I was suicidal. I'd allowed myself to believe a lie: that my family would be better off if I was gone from this earth.

I had to stand toe-to-toe with those feelings and look them in the eye.

I had to accept that they were there—that they were real, and I was feeling them. I had to accept that they were a part of me in those moments. And I learned that shining the light of acceptance on that darkness made it disappear. It helped me embrace all of reality so I could say, "You know what? No one's perfect."

Learning to accept things as they are—and our powerlessness to change them—is how we learn to love ourselves. Accepting imperfections allows for self-compassion and reduces the pressure to constantly strive for unattainable standards.

Accepting Uncertainty

As we learn to accept the things we can't control, we can also learn to accept uncertainty. For me, that's huge. Accepting the nerve disease, complex regional pain syndrome (CRPS), I was diagnosed with—and accepting the fact that I never know how bad the pain is going to be or when a flare-up is going to happen—means embracing uncertainty as an incredibly prevalent force in my life. I often use the Serenity Prayer to help me be in acceptance with that. *God, grant me the serenity to accept the things I cannot change, the courage to change the things I can, and the wisdom to know the difference.*

But look—even if I didn't have CRPS, my world would still be uncertain. I live in Texas, and here we never know if there'll be a tornado one night or a perfect sky or a hailstorm. Beyond weather, there's so much uncertainty in the world today. Recognizing that uncertainty as a natural part of life enables us to embrace the unknown instead of fearing it. We can see it as an opportunity for growth, curiosity, exploration. Through it we can cultivate a sense of openness to new experiences that can actually lead us to greater joy and fulfillment.

Accepting life's fluctuations—and our fluctuating emotions— also builds resilience.

I've learned to accept those fluctuations in emotions. I understand them for what they are: both positive and negative, and ever-changing. Accepting their ebb and flow—without resisting it—can lead to a deeper sense of peace and contentment. In fact, it can also be a reminder: if emotions can fluctuate, I can purposefully build joy even when the pain comes and goes. I don't need to stuff down my emotions when they turn negative, because they will rise no matter what—just like every other emotion.

I don't say that to discount my pain or yours. I want to acknowledge that pain so we can focus our energy on building joy. To do that, we also have to accept our past mistakes.

For example, that terrible Instagram experience I mentioned in the Introduction. After pushing myself too hard and ultimately overdoing it, I had so much shame about appearing so out of it online. I had a really hard time. To get through it, I had to learn how to acknowledge my mistake, accept it, and learn from it—but without dwelling on it or the pain it caused me. That one excruciating experience showed me yet again that accepting my past, including all my regrets and failures, enabled personal growth. And it continues to give me opportunities to move forward with greater will and resilience.

Look—I know self-love is a process. Accepting ourselves for who and what we are—imperfections and mistakes and all—I know that takes time. But I also know that when we commit to it, transformation is possible. Hope is available.

And accepting the uncertainty in our lives—in all its forms—helps us love ourselves better.

Extending Acceptance to Others

I grew up in Texas, in the Bible Belt. There weren't people in my town who looked different from me. We went to church; we went to football games. There was no diversity. I love Texas, but I always felt so different growing up there.

When I moved to Los Angeles there were so many different cultures and religions, so many people and personal beliefs. They all come from a place of love. Experiencing that was a breath of fresh air. I accept and embrace the diversity of perspectives, backgrounds, and beliefs in the world. I *love* that diversity—even when it means my good friend talks smack on Texas and everything Texas is for.

We can all agree to disagree sometimes and accept others for who they are without trying to judge or change them. Instead of dwelling on the differences, how can you learn more about a person's beliefs and who they are? That perspective fosters empathy, connection, and a greater appreciation for the rich human experience.

Extend acceptance to others. We need more of that in our world. Accept differences in others, knowing that not everybody is going to be the same.

It's one more way to cultivate joy in your own life—and spark it in someone else.

Reflection

Acceptance doesn't mean giving up.

Acceptance is freedom. It means that we can accept that something is happening the way it is, or that something exists in our lives, while we simultaneously take action to make our lives better. Acceptance puts you in the driver's seat of your life. It is the key to your true inner power.

It can feel contradictory to admit we're powerless over something so it can make us powerful. But when we're in acceptance, what we think is the hardest thing we've ever gone through or the most shameful experience we've ever had—whether it's a scar on the outside, the inside, or something from our past that still haunts us—can actually be our superpower.

Actionable Steps

Practice mindfulness. "Practice mindfulness" is an easy thing to say. I get that. But for someone like me, it's worth repeating.

For a lot of my life, I didn't even know how much I was *not* in the moment. I was just running away from feelings. Stuffing them down. And then one day I was stuck in a hospital bed and I couldn't run away. When that happened, I was stuck in my feelings, too. I had no tools whatsoever to help me deal. I had to learn how to be mindful.

Meditation can help. If you're a person with kids, they will get you right. With all their "come look at this or thats," they'll snap you right out of your head and right into the moment. Nature walks are effective, and so is focusing on your breathing to come back to the present moment.

There are lots of techniques for breath work, such as box breathing (breathe in, *one two*, breathe out *one two*, breathe in, *one two*, breathe out, *one two*, all while tracing a box shape in the air in time with your breaths). Me, I find it helpful to simply breathe, and when I exhale, take twice as long. Don't try to control it, just allow yourself to breathe. It's amazing the way that simple action puts me right in the moment. As I focus on my breath, I find myself feeling grateful that I have it. Grateful that I get to breathe, right here and right now.

When you practice mindfulness, acceptance comes up. It arises when you acknowledge your thoughts and emotions without judgment and allow them to pass without claiming or resisting them. Allow yourself to have them.

I once heard someone say it's your mind's job to think—and it's really good at thinking. So allow your mind to do its job, allow the thoughts to come up. Then, imagine them like clouds floating away from you and focus on your breath again. That's different from saying, "don't think" or "stop thinking," both of which are impossible to do. No—just let your mind do what it's good at, and then get back to breathing.

Cultivate kindness. I've had a lifetime of mean-talking myself. Do you know that feeling? If I talked to others as meanly as I talk to myself, I would have no friends, no clients, and no one would work with me. That "inner bully" of mine is persistent. But to be kind to myself, I had to learn to put that bully in jail. My bully might always be there, but my job is to put it away and lock the door. Sometimes that inner bully escapes its cell and gets out of jail and comes at me with criticism and negativity. Fine—I just have to lock it back up again by taking those mean words and switching them for caring ones. *How can I be a little nice to myself today?* I ask. *How might I treat myself with kindness?*

This is especially true in challenging times. We need to recognize that imperfections and adversity are all part of being human. Most of us find it easy to extend understanding to someone else, but harder to extend it to ourselves. When I'm sick, I have a tendency to push myself to go go go and keep going, so I can show up for others. But if my daughter was the sick one? I would not tell her to keep going. I would not insist she keep helping others even though she's sick. I would tell her to lie down while I got her some chicken soup. To bring it full circle, cultivating kindness for me is about learning that self-compassion so I can control the aspects of life over which I have the power of influence.

Let go. This is something I practice all the time. For example, I recently had an interview with Google for a speaking gig. I really, really wanted that gig—so much so that I was tempted to sit around and wait for their call afterwards. But what good would that do? I had no control over whether they called me. What could I do instead that would be for me? What could I actually control?

I might not have been able to control whether Google hired me for that gig, but I could be the best coach I could be for my clients. I could devote more of my time to writing this book and pour more of my focus into an upcoming event. Focusing on what I could control enabled me to let go of the things I couldn't. It helped me drift toward actionable steps and personal growth.

(And you know what? Google hired me.)

Seeking support. As you practice acceptance, seek support, ask for help, and keep your support system active. I accepted that I had a problem with alcohol, and the first thing I did when I got sober was to ask someone to help me and take me to a 12-step meeting.

My husband is another support system. Talking to him in the bathroom that night of our anniversary when my leg was so swollen I could barely take my shoe off wasn't the same as a 12-step meeting, but the exchange was no less supportive (it was even a little profound). His comment helped me accept what was happening in the moment. His support helped me maintain my practice of constantly accepting things.

Which helped me a few weeks ago, when I was so excited to go to the gym and do some heavy lifting—and managed to throw out my back before I could leave the house. *Oh, this sucks*, I thought. But amid my mental grumbling, I knew I had to just accept the circumstances. My back was all tweaked—that was happening—and I needed to move forward in acceptance.

That in turn empowered me to explore what I could learn from that particular difficulty. What were the circumstances teaching me? I needed to shift my focus a bit, perhaps, and do more core work to strengthen that area of my body. Maybe I needed to do more reps, or maybe God was trying to tell me something like, "Amberly, you need to slow down. Sure, you're feeling better—but don't go full speed again or else you're going to crash."

Those opportunities we have to learn are hard-won and powerful. Don't let them pass you by.

Key Takeaway

The truth will kick your ass, but then it will set you free.

3

Shift Your Perspective
Serving Others with Gratitude

In the weeks, months, and years following my motorcycle accident, I wanted to make sure I showed appreciation to everyone who supported me.

The instinct to express gratitude was one I'd honed since I was old enough to hold a fat no. 2 pencil and learn my letters in grade school. In fact, I grew up writing thank-you notes for everything. Every single birthday present and every single kindness got a handwritten note of gratitude. *Thank you*, I wrote. Over and over and over.

As you can probably imagine, there were plenty of days in my childhood when writing a thank-you was the *last* thing I wanted to do. But as an adult, I'm grateful for the experience. Growing up with the kind of manners that require you to say "thank you" to anybody and everybody—from teachers to waitresses to faraway relatives who slide a crisp $10 bill into a birthday card—goes a long way.

That was never more apparent than during the stretch of surgeries that followed my accident.

Despite my best efforts to stay positive and focus on healing, I had fallen into a depression. Anyone who has ever had a surgery can probably agree that one is bad enough. Enduring 34 . . . well, it got to me. I couldn't sleep. I was just watching infomercials into the bleak, blue-light drenched hours that stretched between midnight and morning. Nevertheless, I continued writing those thank-you notes . . . and something amazing happened. Expressing my gratitude actually *changed the way I felt.*

Finally, I realized I had a choice. I could continue to spiral down, or I could take the actions that would help me get better. I chose action, and eventually I wound up here. Writing this book for you.

So, I'll say it again: regularly practicing gratitude and showing your appreciation for others goes a *long* way.

That Person You're Thanking Is Not an ATM

A while back, I was invited to guest on Ed Mylett's podcast. If you don't know Ed, well, he is a legend ,and you should check him out! He is someone I have admired and looked up to for years. I met him when we shared the stage at a speaking event and then a few more times when we spoke at other events together. Now let me tell you, Ed is a best-selling author, ranked the number one speaker in the world, and is ranked a number one mindset and performance coach in the world by *USA Today*. I couldn't believe I was going to get to be a guest on his show, *The Ed Mylett Show*, which is ranked top five in the world!! You can understand why I felt like I had won the lottery. This was a dream come true. I was more excited about this opportunity to sit in with Ed than I was when I was asked to be on the *Today Show*, *The Doctors*, or Hallmark just to give you an idea of how excited I was for this interview!

Before we ever started recording, I grabbed the phone to let Ed know how much I appreciated the opportunity.

"I know what a big deal this is," I said, "and I don't take it lightly. I appreciate you. Thank you, thank you, *thank you* for having me on your show—it's like winning the lottery."

I think Ed heard the sincerity in my heart. And when I got to his house a short while later to record the episode, I doubled down on gratitude. I brought a book for his wife (one I knew was specific to her thoughts and beliefs), some gourmet treats for his sweet dogs, and a box of cigars for Ed himself.

"How did you know these were my favorite cigars?" he asked, astonished.

"I didn't," I said, a bit astonished myself. By that time in my life, gratitude in action was such a practice for me that I hadn't given it a second thought beyond wanting Ed to know how much I truly appreciated him.

"Oh, my gosh," he said. "I can't believe you got me this."

Fast-forward to the emails, phone calls, and text messages I received from Ed's listeners after our episode aired. *Oh my gosh* was right. I've never had so many people repost one of my podcast appearances in their story, ever.

I messaged Ed to thank him again, and he told me my episode had more downloads than Tony Robbins's. Tony Robbins! Ed chalked up the overwhelming response to my interview being "the best." But I think he was being nice, and I fully and wholeheartedly believe it was not for any other reason than that I have a real community of friends, Mastermind peers, and even my former therapist in Los Angeles, who were supporting me and sharing the episode across all their platforms.

Each and every person in my community wholeheartedly supports one another, and we show each other we're grateful for that support.

Gratitude is one of our main foundations.

Don't Be a Pimp

People ask me all the time how I'm getting all these amazing speaking gigs. Trust me—no one is more surprised than I am. I'm always shocked when I'm invited to speak at an event.

I'm less surprised when people ask me if I pay for the opportunity to guest on high-profile podcasts. A friend of mine recently asked if that was what happened—had I paid for my episode on Ed Mylett's show?

"No," I answered. "I've built that relationship for years."

My friend followed up with, "How did you do that?"

"I've never asked him for anything," I said. "I've just appreciated him and brought value to him by sharing his posts. I supported his book, and I didn't do it expecting something in return. I genuinely wanted to build the relationship."

I'll admit that's not typically how people expect things to work. A quid pro quo—you scratch my back, I'll scratch yours—is the unspoken rule of "networking," and that leaves a bad taste, doesn't it? Take, for example, a recent interaction I had with a friend of mine (whom I dearly love). She saw me interviewing Jaime Kern Lima of IT Cosmetics on my podcast and called me up forthwith.

Before I tell you about the call, I should tell you that my face was busted up when I did that interview. There I was, speaking to the flawlessly gorgeous Jaime Kern Lima, and then the camera would pan to me, with my two black eyes and stitches on my forehead from head butting our coffee table while horsing around with Ruby. Surely some god of humor, somewhere out there in the ether, cooked up that particular visual contrast. I can imagine my viewers' thoughts: *Holy crap, what happened to her?*

So after the episode aired, I heard from my friend. *Oh, Amberly*, she messaged, *I'm really concerned about you. Are you doing okay? Do I need to come out there and just hug you? Anyway, I was wondering—can you introduce me to . . .* and she proceeded to name several high-profile people I'd worked with, including Jaime.

Far be it for me to assume I know anyone's motives. But when I read the message, I felt like *ohhhh-kay. That's why you're really reaching out. You want me to introduce you to the people I've spent years developing relationships with.*

But I respect them, so I'm not going to pimp them out.

I invite you to flip the script on networking, from *what can they do for me* to *what can I do for somebody else*? Build relationships for the sake of the relationship itself. Help someone else for the joy and success it will bring to them, full stop. Train yourself to be motivated by someone else's success instead of just your own.

Trust me, what you'll get in return is *so much better* than a leg up on your competition. Again, I'm talking about community—not one full of associates, but one of true friends.

That's what happened when Kathryn Gordon joined my Mastermind group. Kathryn is the best-selling author of *Relationship Grit*, which she coauthored with her husband, Jon. She is an executive movie producer and the most amazing mother of two beautiful children. I knew her, and her husband, Jon Gordon, from the time they graciously appeared on my podcast. Afterward I learned that Kathryn was ready to start speaking and podcasting on her own, so I helped her with everything I could. I wasn't expecting anything in return. I just really loved her and believed in all her big dreams. Now she is speaking on stages across the country and has a top podcast called "*Kathryn For Real*" thanks to all her hard work.

Over the next two years, Kathryn and I became the best of friends. I've never asked anything of her or Jon, but that didn't stop Jon from noticing how much Kathryn had done with the advice and strategies I'd given her. He offered to come and speak at one of my events to support me.

Of course I was dying—THE ONE AND ONLY Jon Gordon—and of course I was a little stunned. I had watched Jon's talks for years and admired and studied his work. He is a top three speaker in the world on leadership and number one consultant to some of the biggest companies in the world including the NFL and NBA. I had been listening to his amazing podcast, *The Jon Gordon Show*, for years (and even got to be a guest, by the way). I have every single one of his 31 books, 17 of which are best-sellers! By the time this book comes out he will probably have 40 books. So I was on top of the world and a little in disbelief that he would be speaking at one of my events.

Now, I have to say, I've witnessed this kind of thing over and over in my life, but it still floors me sometimes when simple, genuine appreciation and friendship result in reciprocal appreciation—and this was just like that.

See, there's an ebb and flow to appreciation and gratitude. I expressed mine for Kathryn, and she became my friend. Jon expressed appreciation and gratitude by speaking at my event. And I expressed my appreciation and gratitude for that gesture by buying his best-selling book *One Truth*—for every single attendee at my event.

Reflection

For me, gratitude in action looks like continually expressing gratitude with your heart firmly in the right place. It isn't, "how will saying thank you eventually support me," but "how can I support this person in who they are and what they're doing?" I've never asked Ed Mylett for anything, but I did want to support him—and now I have the privilege of calling him my friend. That means more to me than any number of podcast appearances or speaking gigs.

Here's another way of saying all that: do *not* practice gratitude so you can get stuff.

That doesn't mean it won't happen. Promotions, opportunities, and open doors can (and often do) come as a by-product of showing your appreciation for someone. Wonderful. But getting those things—or anything else—from someone should never be your motivation for appreciating them. Don't say "thank you" because you think it will help you level up.

Why? Because gratitude in action is capable of *so much more* than moving your career forward.

Letting someone know they're truly appreciated—and that you're not just after them for something—develops trust. So whether it's a thank-you note, a gift, appreciating your Starbucks barista or customer service representative over the phone, express your gratitude *and mean it*. Give someone that gift and watch their energy change from negative to positive.

You'll increase their joy, and that makes it all worthwhile.

And in the process, you might even spark more joy for yourself.

Not too long ago, I connected with an amazing female entrepreneur who has a very high-end home fragrance line. She told me on a call that she had decided to donate 50 units of her company's diffusers to people who were coming to one of my events. I was so grateful for the gift that I started crying right there on the phone with her as I expressed my appreciation.

"I looked at your story," she said, "and I know that you were a single mom for a long time. You really built your business as a single mom—and I did, too." By that time, we were both crying.

"I'm going to put something together for your event and make it really special," she continued.

My appreciation for her generosity forged a deeper, more genuine connection between us. I told her afterwards that we were going to be friends for life—and I believe we will be. I've seen it happen so many times in my own life that I know it to be true.

Here's another example. A few years ago, a friend of mine made an introduction that landed me a high-paying speaking gig, and I thanked her by putting together a very specific, personalized collection of gifts that I personally chose and shopped for. She appreciated it so much that she now refers me to everyone, everywhere. But really, the referrals are beside the point. This wonderful woman has become one of my best friends, and having her in my life brings me joy.

I could keep going all day about all the friends I've made after expressing gratitude. In so many instances, it all started with a heartfelt expression of thanks.

Plain and simple.

Actionable Steps

Gratitude journaling. People talk about gratitude and gratitude journaling all the time, but let me tell you—it really works. When you want to shift your perspective, gratitude journaling is a great place to start.

It's one thing to read books—that's when we learn about each other (and it's great to learn from other people and about other places). Journaling is an entirely different thing. When you journal, you learn about *yourself*.

Journaling specifically about gratitude is a game changer. I promise it'll help shift your focus from what's lacking in your life to what you have. It will foster a sense of abundance and appreciation. Do it first thing in the morning and it'll start your day off great. Heck, it'll change your whole mood. When you're in gratitude, you can't be sad. You simply can't be grateful and sad at the same time because gratitude sparks joy.

Dedicate time each day to write down the things you're grateful for, and reflect on the positive aspects of your life. No matter how small, consider how they contribute to your well-being.

Express appreciation. Make a habit of expressing gratitude to those around you. Take time to thank people for the positive ways they've affected your life. Genuine expressions of gratitude strengthen relationships and create another ripple effect of positivity.

This isn't something I've learned from a book. I don't have a PhD in joy, resilience, or grit. But I have decades' worth of life experience that has shown me what works and what doesn't.

Random acts of kindness and service. Recently, I had a client that complained about being bored. "I just don't feel fulfilled," she said.

"Why don't you go help somebody?" I suggested. "Go volunteer."

Practicing generosity can increase feelings of gratitude and fulfillment, which also spark joy.

So if you're sad, go help somebody.

If you're frustrated, go help somebody.

If you're feeling sorry for yourself, *go help somebody*.

You don't have to have everything figured out. You don't have to have everything together. Just volunteer your time somewhere, offer a listening ear to someone who needs it, or buy coffee for a stranger in line at Starbucks.

I did a version of that when I first moved back to Texas from California. It was late; my daughter Ruby and I had been moving boxes and unpacking all day. We were exhausted. We were trying to find a place nearby to get dinner—something that would've been relatively easy in Los Angeles, where you can always find something to eat. But in our new, smaller Texas town, we weren't having any luck. I drove around and drove around, the day wearing on me.

Finally, I found a Whataburger. We went through the drive-through, and I was just *so tired*. When I paid for our meal, I decided to also pay for the guy behind us, too. *I'll never see the guy*, I thought, *but I'll make his day a little*. Plus, I knew it would make me feel good to help someone else.

Food in hand, I pulled over and found a parking space where Ruby and I could sit and eat in the car. I sort of forgot that I'd paid for someone else's dinner until a truck pulled up beside us on the passenger's side and rolled its window down. The guy inside just looked at us. Down went Ruby's window.

"Oh, my gosh," the driver of the truck said, "thank you so much. That was the nicest thing. You just made my day."

People remember those small acts of kindness. With any luck, it's like dropping a stone into a pond, sending a ripple effect of even more kindness out into the world. Maybe that guy was inspired to do something for someone else, and someone else, and someone else.

And maybe that sparked joy for hundreds, even thousands of people . . . miles away from that Whataburger.

It's like someone once said: "Speaking kindly to plants helps them grow. Imagine what speaking kindly to humans can do."

Shift from me to we. Recognize the interconnectedness of all beings and the impact of your actions on others instead of solely focusing on personal gain. Take a hard look at your choices and behaviors. How might they benefit the greater good?

Above all, act for the good of others *without expecting anything in return*. That's the key.

Mahatma Gandhi said, "The best way to find yourself is to lose yourself in the service of others." My friend Les Brown says, "Help others achieve your dreams and you'll achieve yours." Service is such a mindset of abundance. It's where the magic is. Helping someone is where you spark joy.

That's why I share everything I do with others. My Mastermind group often comments on it. "Wow, you really share everything you really do," they'll say. And I do. I open up my little black book of strategies for success and share it all. I want to see others succeed, so I'll tell anyone who'll listen everything I've done that's helped me along the way. Being of service to others and their success is where you truly find fulfillment, and it sure sparks joy!

Helping someone else succeed gives me more joy than my own success. Their successes don't mean there's less for me. I think if people—especially women—realized that if they came together in collaboration instead of competition, they wouldn't believe the results. There's enough success, enough opportunity.

For everybody.

Practice presence. When we moved to Texas from California, and bought a lovely house with two hammocks in the backyard, life was nonstop. In the middle of all that chaos—and maybe, partially, this *caused* the chaos—we had moved tons and tons of boxes, and we were trying to unpack them all.

In fact, a typical morning for me went something like this: *Oh, shoot, Ruby has to go to school early. I have to make her lunch, and I'm still in my robe. And I have a client at eight o'clock. And I'm going to show up in my robe . . . after I take Ruby to school, still in my robe . . .*

Then one day, I finally went out to the backyard to sit in one of the hammocks.

I took a breath and gazed up at our beautiful new home.

And I started to cry.

In that first moment of being in the present since the move, I realized that I'd been able to put a roof over my family's head. That was no small feat, because at one point I'd accumulated $2.9 million in medical expenses and, as a result, the bank had a lien on our house. But that day I could admit that it had taken years, but I was able to buy our Texas home. *Look at all that hard work I've done*, I thought. *Look what I've accomplished.*

In that moment, I was fully engaged in the present. I was able to savor the experience.

Sometimes, it takes slowing down and appreciating the richness of life, the interactions, the encounters, to deepen your gratitude and connection to others. It doesn't have to be looking at a big house. It could be walking into nature and appreciating that winter is coming to an end and flowers are beginning to appear. It could be looking up at the sky and appreciating that simple pleasure—to breathe and walk outside.

Whatever your moment is, locate your place in it and be still. Let it wash over you and hit home. If you're like me even a little bit, you'll think, *Wow. I have so much to be grateful for.*

Key Takeaway

Gratitude changes what you can't do into what you can and what you don't have into what you do. It's my medicine.

4

Forgiveness

The Liberating Journey to Emotional Freedom

If you read my first book, you know there are a lot of people in my life I've needed to forgive. First on that list was my dad, who didn't do anything to stop my stepdad from sexually abusing me after I told him about the abuse.

I loved my dad then and I love him now. But for years, I felt hurt and unworthy. I became anything and everything I thought would make Dad proud. That desire got me to graduate with top honors, got me named Miss Greenville High School, got me into state competitions for the gifted and talented program—and won me a state championship in that competition to boot. I choreographed for the cheer team and did all these extracurricular activities while working two jobs. I was such an overachiever, and I did it all because I was screaming for Dad's approval. It was the one thing I *didn't* get.

I eventually accepted my feelings of unworthiness and hurt. When I did, I found that the way Dad handled the situation enabled my trial-by-fire early years to teach me things. Because I had no help or true escape, I learned how to be self-reliant. To defend myself. That a road of pain and fear could lead me to Muay Thai boxing and push me to California and a successful career in dance. And, because I strove for Dad's approval and never got it, I learned to approve of myself. Hardship really taught me that I was *capable* of all those things. That I could take care of and love myself.

But forgiving my Dad went so much deeper than physical fitness or dance. I had to let go.

Before I could do that, I had to learn that letting go starts with forgiveness.

Forgiving Dad meant I needed to remind myself of a few things. First of all, that I loved him despite all the pain. Second, that when I looked at things through the lens of my love, I had empathy and compassion for him. I could recognize that he was living with his own trauma from childhood. His mother was an alcoholic; he grew up in poverty, felt abandoned, and was never given the right tools to handle any of it. Maybe that's why he's so good at keeping secrets. Tell my Dad something and he'll take it to the grave.

Thinking about that brought me to another realization: Dad actually *did* try to help me. He just did it in the exact way I'd asked him to. I made him promise not to tell anyone what was happening to me, and he kept that promise thinking it was the best way he could help me. It wasn't—but that doesn't change that he tried.

I have a lot of compassion for people who've experienced something horrible at someone else's hand and are just getting through it. I lived that life. Sometimes you have to learn to forgive later.

Stepping into forgiveness for my Dad was not a quick or easy thing. For a long time, I shoved down any thoughts of forgiveness—especially while I was in full-on survival mode. All I could think of in those years was that I always needed to be ready to fight off my stepdad. *How am I going to be okay? What the next steps I can take to make sure I take care of myself, get stronger, and keep this from happening again?* Those were the only thoughts I really had. If I'd focused on being upset with my real dad, I wouldn't have been able to take action and move forward.

Finally, though, I did move forward. Part of that process included writing my first book, *True Grit and Grace*. In it, I made no bones about the fact that Dad didn't come to my rescue. My feelings were right there in his face.

He came to me, crying. And for the first time, he apologized.

By that time, I was 48 years old, and I'd done the work to forgive him years before he ever showed up with tears streaking his cheeks. And it left me free, in my heart and my head, to voice a beautiful truth.

"Dad," I said, "I forgave you a long time ago."

Faith Fortifies Us in Forgiveness

So how does that forgiveness relate to my joy? After healing the relationship with my dad, our bond is stronger. We talk more. I no longer feel the way I did when I was the middle child, striving for his attention through accomplishments and high grades at school.

Forgiving Dad also nudged me toward my own healing through years of letting go, of therapy, of reading books of faith and having God as my higher power. Instead of feeling like I needed a dad to keep me safe, I thought, *You know what? I always have a God who is stronger than any of my circumstances—a God I can always rely on because he walks with me no matter where I go.*

That faith has carried me so far. To this day it's what gives me peace and enables me to spark joy. I have serenity because I know I can trust my higher power.

Actually, let's talk about faith for a moment. I grew up in a God-fearing home, in a God-fearing town, in a God-and-country state. I heard "The devil made you do that" any time I made a mistake, or "God's watching you" any time an adult thought I was *about* to make one (always followed by, "You're going to get punished"). In my town—in my house—you did not miss church. *Ever.*

I remember being in a car accident on Saturday night when I was 16. I broke my leg and had a bad concussion. I woke up Sunday morning throwing up; my leg was swollen and purple. Mom came into my room like clockwork, dressed in her Sunday best.

"Get up," she said. "We have to go to church."

I looked down at my leg. "Mom, I can't put pantyhose over my leg. I can't even *walk*."

She must've seen that I was basically on my deathbed—the only reason missing church was allowed—because she said, "I guess you can skip this time."

In my experience, that's what God-fearing was. I have since come to believe God-fearing is different than faith.

When I was young, I felt comfort when I was in church. As an adult, I still do. When I go to church with my grandmother, I still love singing (or lip-singing) from the hymnals; I love the Lord's Prayer and all the things I grew up with. But sometimes I felt different back then. The place I felt most *connected* with God wasn't in church at all—it was when I was out in nature. I felt especially close when I ran track. I talked to God with every lap around the track, with every footfall, with every breath.

Whatever your God or your higher power is, we all need one to give us the strength and resilience to get through the really tough challenges we'll face in this life. Lean into that guiding presence in your life as you work through and build back.

And let's face it: forgiving someone who's wronged us can be one of those challenges. It can feel good, in the moment at least, to hold on to anger and resentment. Sometimes it seems easier to stuff down our feelings of pain, shame, jealousy— whatever negative ick is weighing you down. Believe me, I know. Like I said before, I stuffed away every bad feeling and experience. I compartmentalized. I held on tight until everything came crumbling down around me—because *I just couldn't do it anymore.*

When that happened, I had to learn to look at those feelings, address them, and ask myself the right questions to help me get through.

It's All About Empowerment, Chicks

I have always wanted to feel empowered.

Ever since I was a little girl, before I ever even knew the word—let alone what it meant—I wanted empowerment for myself. An early attempt at it had me starting a club with my girl cousins. We called ourselves the Super Chicks, and I was President Chick, and I made t-shirts with fuzzy baby chicks on them and everything. Sounds cute, right? Well, I started the club because our boy cousins liked to be mean to us. When it happened, we convened meetings of the Chicks in the chicken coop at my grandmother's house and planned out what we would do the next time they tried to get us.

As I got older, I taught myself a different path to empowerment. It starts with getting really quiet. I look inside and ask, *What do I think and feel? What are my options?* In other words, I start figuring out what's true and right for me.

When it comes to empowerment, personal truth is incredibly important. But look—it can't stop there. You have to pair that honesty with your *options*. Why? Because options are our path to action.

Things get hard sometimes, and action can seem impossible. I know plenty of people who feel like they've run out of options at one time or another. But I'm here to tell you that no matter what your situation is, no matter what you're feeling, you always have another option. There is always another way through or around.

Take my youngest daughter, Ruby, for example. Ruby is always thinking—oftentimes, about how badly she wants to raise chickens. She's wanted them all her life, but our home owners association just will not allow them. So she started exploring options.

"Mom, we could hide them," she said to her dad and me one day.

"You can't hide chickens," Johnny said. "How are you going to hide chickens?"

"Well," I said, "we could at least see if it's *possible*."

After exploring possibilities, Ruby concluded that her dad was right. It wasn't going to work. But she also discovered a new breed of chickens to dote on that are smaller and easier to keep. And that sent her down a new path of hopeful planning (and maybe a little harmless scheming). Perhaps they'll be an option for her in the future—something she can work toward.

In the face of zero chicken options, Ruby empowered herself to create new ones.

Forgiveness and Emotional Empowerment

From an emotional perspective, the process I walk through to empower myself is very much the same as what Ruby did with her hypothetical chickens.

When I am shaking-hands nervous—like I can get before I speak at an event—I talk myself through my options to help me switch that negative energy into a positive place. First I have to ask myself questions and get clarity so I'm able to recognize important things about what I'm feeling. *Where are these feelings coming from?* I ask. *Are they true for me? Is this a feeling or is it reality?* Homing in on those answers frees me to say, *This feeling can be excitement, too, because this talk isn't about me. It's about the people I serve.*

All of this brings us back to forgiveness—and, just as important, how to handle or redirect our own negative feelings into a path forward. I do this all the time. And look—I don't want anyone thinking that I never get upset. I have a long fuse, but when it's gone . . . well. Just ask my husband, who'll look at me and say, "Okay, okay, Amberly. Don't go all Texas on me." I get upset plenty, but I've learned to really *look* at my anger and frustration, my disappointment and pain. I feel the feelings, examine them, and address them.

Being in that practice *before* my motorcycle accident meant I didn't allow anger to overrule my healing process *afterward.* By that time, I'd become adept at focusing on my options. In fact, I was so focused on what I could do to heal, both physically and emotionally, that although I wondered briefly why the driver who hit me with his SUV never came to the hospital, I was otherwise too busy moving forward to be overcome with anger. I knew I could wallow in bad feelings, sure. But I also knew I couldn't have that kind of energy. I knew if I stayed in anger or resentment, it would eat me up. I wouldn't have healed the way that I did.

So instead, I focused on the gratitude I had for being alive. I focused on living, on saving my leg through the next surgery, and on what I could do to make that happen, like controlling my blood sugar levels so I didn't need to take insulin and risk further infection. And I focused on how I could stay connected to God every single day, sometimes every *moment* of every single day. In other words, I focused on anything and everything I could do to be better mentally, physically, spiritually, and emotionally.

And do you know what happened? Not only did I heal but I also began to feel compassion for the man who hit me. *Wow,* I thought, *I would almost rather be in the hospital than having to live with the knowledge that I had harmed someone else. What must he feel?*

Maybe he felt nothing. It's possible. Me, I don't know if I could've lived with that kind of guilt. If he felt even a small bit of it, as I suspected he might, I had compassion for that. And whether he felt anything or not, that compassion helped me see that I also had forgiveness.

It was such a gift.

For myself.

Free Yourself to Take Back Your Power

Forgiveness is what we do for ourselves. It's freedom from suffering *for us.*

That's how forgiveness liberates joy. Giving someone grace or letting go of that past hurt brings about a sense of freedom, joy, and happiness. It releases you from the emotional burden of baggage, anger, and resentment. It's not about being selfless. It's about creating a pathway to perfect peace and emotional well-being.

The journey to forgiveness is really a journey of self-discovery. It's a conscious choice to let go and accept release.

I think a lot of people put all their focus on what's bad about the things that happen. But imagine what could happen if, instead, they released their grip on that negativity and just focused on, "Well, what's next? What are my choices?"

Excusing others' actions when they've wronged us doesn't mean you're condoning things they've done. It's simply means freeing ourselves of the need or compulsion to *focus* on that anger and resentment. That, in turn, allows us to reclaim our power and control of our emotions. Then, we can assert that reclaimed power over the way we feel—and *that's* how we take the power back from someone else. It keeps us from giving another person so much influence over our thoughts, emotions, and life.

Holding on to anger is bad enough, but holding on to resentment might be worse. In fact it's been shared in recovery meetings that resentment is the number one emotion that will lead people to break their sobriety. That's how powerful it is.

If you're holding on to resentment, you are going to make bad decisions. You're going to slip into old addictions or old habits. If you don't let it go, it will destroy your life. It's like that old saying: refusing to forgive somebody for something is like drinking poison yourself and expecting them to die.

But by embracing forgiveness and letting go of resentment, we free ourselves from the shackles of the past so we can embrace a future filled with possibility and joy.

Reflection

Learning to forgive is not always easy. It requires courage and compassion. We have to confront our pain for so long, acknowledge our emotions, and choose to release the grip of negativity over and over again.

I mentioned in previous chapters that we have to cultivate empathy and compassion toward ourselves and others. Personally,

I had to cultivate that compassion and empathy for the man who didn't protect me. It opened the door to letting go, which opened the door to the forgiveness, which enabled my father and me to have a meaningful relationship. We have a deeper connection, a deeper understanding of each other. We can talk about anything.

When the strain left our relationship, the stress went with it.

That's what happens when we clear out all that emotional gunk, when we take back control of how we feel. And we should do that. I'm a firm believer that anger and resentment take a toll on a person's physical body, sometimes manifesting as cancer, high blood pressure, or other illnesses.

But when we get rid of all that negativity, we're free to seek out our purpose.

Actionable Steps

Acknowledge your emotions. Pain, anger, resentment—whatever that hurt is, look it straight in the eye and acknowledge it. Taking that pause often enables us to recognize the person or situation we need to forgive. It isn't easy. In fact, it might be really hard. But it's important because it's the only way you're truly going to heal. Truth will kick your ass a little bit, but then it'll set you free.

Make the effort to understand the other perspective. Sometimes that's not an easy one, either. Me, I had to understand the circumstances of the person who hurt me, and use that understanding to develop empathy for them. Empathy and compassion go hand-in-hand with forgiveness.

Set boundaries. If I'm being completely honest, I don't know if I've totally forgiven my stepfather for the sexual abuse. But I did set healthy boundaries to protect myself from being hurt again.

- Boundaries can be physical, like the miles I put between us when I moved to California or the times I didn't come home at night while I had to live under the same roof as him.

- Boundaries can also be set around our time. When there's a person in our life who is draining, we need to put limits on how much time we're spending with them. (I'll talk about that more in Chapter 8.)

- Boundaries can mean letting a relationship go entirely. Sometimes you gotta just bless 'em and block 'em.

Realize that forgiveness is a choice—and then choose it. Understanding forgiveness as a choice helps us *decide* to release the need for resentment. Choosing forgiveness brings peace of mind. We can choose to let the anger and resentment fester inside us, or we can choose to let it go and focus on what's next (or even what you can do to help another person who has been through the same thing).

Focus on self-healing. Engage in activities and focus on things that promote your healing and self-care. For me, that was journaling and therapy. If your finances won't allow for traditional therapy, there are programs that offer it for free. Therapy podcasts are another great source. You can learn from a therapist just by listening and practicing mindfulness.

Be part of a group. I think one of the most healing things you can do—and that really aids forgiveness—is being with a circle of people who understand you and your experiences. For me, that was women who were sober. When you're with your people, you have access to deeper understanding, feelings of being connected, and a sense of belonging. Find your inner circle— that place you belong—and be vulnerable with the people in it. Like Brent Brown says, "Vulnerability is the essence of connection and the birthplace of belonging."

Practice patience and persistence. Because forgiveness isn't always easy, we need to be persistent and patient with ourselves as we let go of negative emotions. Learning to give ourselves grace is really practicing empathy for ourselves and honoring our efforts. And let's face it—sometimes, the person we need to forgive is *us*. I know I've had to forgive myself for a lot of things. That's perfectly normal.

I'll repeat something I said in Chapter 2: treat yourself with the same empathy and understanding that you would extend to a friend going through a similar situation. Think of it this way: if a friend said they'd made a mistake, let somebody down, or lost their temper with their kids or husband, most of us would say, "Hey, we all go through that. We're human."

Say the same thing to *you*.

Key Takeaway

Forgiveness is what we do for ourselves. It's freedom from suffering for us.

5

The Power of Mindful Living

Finding Joy in the Present Moment and
Celebrating Everyday Achievements
Along the Way

About the time I gave my first TED Talk, I basically had blinders on to life. I didn't realize it then, but on the drive from Los Angeles to Berkeley, California, I didn't celebrate anything.

And you'd think I would celebrate, right? You'd think I'd be elated all the way north, that I'd be taking everything in. But I don't remember any of the scenery from that road trip. I don't think I even looked out the window—really *looked*—a single time as Johnny drove. All I was looking at was my notes and slides as I practiced my talk over and over and over in my head. I was laser focused on that talk—and the fact that I would be on a stage, speaking in front of 2,500 people, and I would be the only person up there without a PhD.

We finally got to Berkeley, and I got onstage for my mock run. As I practiced giving my talk and clicking through the slides that went with it, I realized I had a problem. One slide had a list of 13 different ways I'd tried to alleviate my chronic pain, and I had to click through all of them without accidentally jumping too far and landing on the next slide before I was ready. *Thank God I got to do a rehearsal,* I thought. *I would've really screwed up with these slides.*

Afterward, Johnny and Ruby went out to explore Berkeley—to see the town, go out to dinner. Me? I was in our tiny little hotel room, prepping. I paced back-and-forth, I practiced clicking 13 times on my clicker, I talked it through again and again. I never even *saw* Berkeley, let alone had the opportunity to enjoy it. And I was so hyper-focused on not screwing up my TED Talk that I couldn't enjoy the fact that I was there to give one in the first place.

That didn't change after I gave my talk the next day. I felt good about it, but as the adrenaline faded, the pain from complex regional pain syndrome started kicking in. I was about to be in a world of hurt. So for the reception afterward, I swapped out the strappy shoes with their two-inch heels I'd worn onstage for my trusty, comfortable boots. I entered the reception wearing them, and was approached by a woman almost immediately.

If I'd hoped to hear a congratulations or compliment come out of her mouth, I was about to be sorely disappointed. She also experienced a lot of pain, the result of an autoimmune disease. "If you've really got pain," she demanded to know, "how could you wear those shoes onstage?"

"Well, I've got boots on right now," I said, "and those heels were only two inches high. But yes—it did hurt. That's why I'm wearing old boots with my dress now." I then also explained, as if I really needed to give her any explanation, that my ankle is actually fused and I have to have a shoe with a little lift in order to even walk properly.

I now wear boots with a two-inch heel all the time, even to work out at the gym. In fact, a fella came over to me at the gym the other day and said, "I'm not sure you are aware of this but your nickname here at the gym is Boots."

Anyway . . .

Here we are at a reception, I thought, *and that's what you have to say to me?* There's a famous quote that says people who *aren't* in the arena will always want to tell you how you didn't do a good job or come down on you or judge you. But until that person gets in the arena themselves and are covered in its blood, sweat, and tears, their opinion doesn't matter. *Sorry,* I thought, looking at the woman who'd just verbally assaulted me, *but you just don't get it.*

The woman *harrumphed* in dismissal and that was that. Me, I was no closer to enjoying the moment than I'd been before giving my talk. I moved on to the next conversation and the next and the next, blinders firmly in place.

I remember getting in the car to go home and immediately calling my videographer. I'd paid him, flown him to Berkeley, and put him up in a hotel room so that he could video my talk and get pictures of me onstage. I said, "Did you get the shot?" meaning, *Did you get a photo of me standing in the middle of that stage on that infamous red circle in front of 2,500 people?*

"Well," he said, "no. I didn't get it."

In fact, Ruby—who was 11—got better video than he did, and hers was the footage I ended up using on social media. At the time, all I could think was, *Well, it's too late now. I have to move on to my next talk.* And so I started prepping for that 45-minute keynote as any excitement I might have felt over my TED Talk slipped through my fingers.

And once again, I didn't even look out the window all the way home.

Full Throttle Versus Full Potential

During that period of my life, it wasn't unusual to hear my husband say, "Oh my gosh, Amberly. When are things going to slow down?"

"I promise you they are going to," I'd respond. But it seemed like everything kept speeding up. I was following the advice of my publicist, who told me at the very beginning of my speaking career to say yes to everything. It was good advice and I followed it. But years later, I was still saying yes to every opportunity. I was still at full throttle.

There are those seasons, I thought. *They're necessary to get us where we want to go.* But I finally had to stop and consider whether I was still in a season or if I had made "full throttle" my new reality. I asked myself, *Where's my life balance? Is there really any kind of life balance?* and *What patterns am I creating that I would rather not repeat in the future? What's helping me and what's hurting me? Where am I not living my full potential?*

Because the truth was, I might've been living my full work potential. I'd just done a TED Talk. I'd been asked to be on *The Doctors*. The Hallmark Channel wanted to interview me, and I was going to be featured in *USA Today*. In my mind, I was like, *accomplishment, accomplishment, accomplishment.* I was checking off the boxes. I was crossing things off my career bucket list. And then one day I was on the phone with my dad, telling him about all these great accomplishments. "Guess what I'm doing now?" I said. "Something big just happened."

Dad didn't respond the way I thought he would.

He didn't say, "Wow—congratulations!" or "Oh my gosh, that's so awesome. I'm so proud of you!" Nope, there was none of that. Instead, he said, "Well, just don't forget to enjoy the journey."

It stopped me in my tracks.

That moment hit me so hard—hard enough to make me pull back and ask if I actually *was* enjoying the journey. Was this what I really wanted, or was I just living life on autopilot and doing the next thing?

Because the other part of my truth was that I wasn't living up to my full potential for my family. I wasn't around for them the way I wanted to be. I also wasn't living up to my full potential in taking care of myself. All that was on the back burner.

When I realized all that, I also got quiet and asked myself the same questions I talked about in Chapter 4: *What do I think? What do I feel? What are my options?*

What I thought was this: my kids needed me when they were little, but I've always felt that when they became teenagers they needed me a little more. I'm lucky enough that my 16-year-old, Ruby, still wants me around—and I want to be around for her. While I was working on this book, she asked me one day to go to the lake with a couple of her friends. *Well, hell,* I thought, *if she wants me to go, I'm going to go.*

So, we went to the lake. While Ruby and her friends paddle-boarded, I walked up a little hill by myself to some railroad tracks. "I'm going for a walk," I said to the girls, thinking I'd give them a little time to themselves.

Five minutes later, I heard footsteps behind me. I turned around and sure enough, there were the girls, following me down the train tracks. I walked back and met up with them, and then we kept walking and talking the whole way. They confided in me, and I felt so grateful that they felt safe to tell me things. In fact, one of the girls even said, "Wow, Ruby! You actually told your mom about that?" I feel so blessed that Ruby does feel safe to tell me things that the other girls apparently would never tell their parents. Ruby and I never even thought it was a big deal to share these things.

I want as many of those kind of moments as I can get in this life. And I knew that even before my dad threw me for a loop by telling me to make sure I enjoyed my life. But his comment enabled me to make changes along the way, like traveling less and staying home more, that help me have the life I want most of all.

I always say it's okay to go fast on the straightaways, but you gotta slow down on the curves. If you don't, you'll crash. Maybe even get emotionally burned out.

It's so critical to take the blinders off, to look up and around, and ask ourselves what's important to us. When I don't do that, my whole world shrinks down to the four walls of my tiny office. I'm just staring at a screen or a piece of paper while I'm totally focused on this keynote or that one. Forever.

In that world, I lose track of what's important, like sitting in the back seat of a car with Ruby and eating a box of our favorite cookies. In that world—and it comes on fast, believe me—to-do lists and checking boxes and accomplishing things fly at me so fast and furious that I can't stop to enjoy them before they become my routine. My normal. What I think *all* of my life is.

But in that place, I am missing so much.

I'm missing the way I felt on that walk up the hill from the lake, that sense of relief and peace and joy and freedom that came from being outside, feeling the sun on my face, smelling fresh air, and hearing the laughter of my daughter and her friends. I'm missing the perfect clarity and understanding that only comes in those moments: *this is what life is supposed to be about.*

People ask me all the time—especially on podcasts—what success looks like to me. I tell them success is being able to do things that you love with the people whom you love. That's when we reach our full potential. By that measure, I'm successful. I love my daughters. I love the women in my Mastermind. I love the speakers who speak alongside me at my events. I love Johnny and our strong marriage and the life we get to live together with our family.

I might not have any of that if I hadn't learned to let go.

Grace over Control

It wasn't until I got sober that I realized what a control freak I've always been. The trauma and abuse I suffered from such a young age left me with the sense that everything around me was out of control. It began with my parents' divorce and the fact that we never had any money. Then came the sexual abuse from my stepdad and the physical abuse from my brother. It all added up.

So I thought, *If I get four jobs, I'll control how much money I have. If I control how much I exercise and how much I eat, I'll control the outcome of that track meet and how I'll win that race. If I train harder than everybody else, I'll control the way I look.* Looking back, I probably had a borderline eating disorder because I was trying so hard to control anything I could.

And then, when I got older, I couldn't control how much I drank or how fast I accomplished certain things. Eventually I realized I was completely out of control—and once I felt like I needed to control my drinking and couldn't, I admitted my powerlessness over my addiction and found freedom. I was finally able to free myself and turn my attention to areas that I could control: my mindset.

See, it really opened up a place in my life that enabled God to be my guiding presence—a source of safety and comfort. It was more powerful than anything, and it gave me peace and serenity to know that I didn't *have* to control everything. God was the one controlling it all, and all I had to do was be saved and loyal and ask for guidance and direction.

Knowing there was that power greater than me, I could finally take a breath. I didn't feel alone. I didn't feel like I had to keep gritting it out. I didn't feel like I had to control any-thing. I had the grace of God, and that meant I could loosen my grip. I could trust when things didn't work out exactly the way I thought they should.

And I felt like I had joy.

Look—there have been so many times in my life when I should have died. My motorcycle accident. The time I became septic and one more day of waiting to go to the hospital would have killed me (that story is coming in a later chapter). In recov-ery, when I was taking so much pain medication after surgery and drank alcohol on top of it and was lucky to wake up the next morning.

My husband likes to say, "God just keeps spitting you back out. Only God knows when it's your time." I agree—and the only thing I'll add is that God has a plan. Through everything in my life, my loving God has continued to say, "No, it's not yet your time."

Knowing all that, and giving up control, took away the need to push, push, push and to check boxes all the time. It freed me to pay attention to my life. To look around and be in those beautiful moments I described previously.

Finding Freedom

As soon as I stopped putting energy into controlling everything—including other people and events—I could start investing more energy into taking care of myself. Because look—it is not our job to manage other people. I can't control what someone thinks or says about me. But I can focus on sparking joy wherever and whenever possible. And I can only strive to increase my energy in that area as long as I don't get caught up in self-will or pushing against something immovable. I have to let all that go so I can flow with the life around me and in me.

There's a saying in recovery: *turn it over, let go, and let God.* But the truth is, I was in fight or flight for a long time. I ran from problems or I fought them. I told myself I just had to grit it out, time after time after time. And I lived in this place where I felt like I had no other option than to just keep going.

I think a lot of people—especially women—are stuck trying to hold it all together. We're trying to hold our emotions together because there's still a stigma if we cry that we'll look out of control, or that we'll be called crazy or weak. We have years, even decades of socialization telling us *I have to be the best mom. I have to be the best wife. I have to be the top leader of my company and keep it together.*

For me, that meant keeping up appearances. On the outside, I looked put together, but on the inside, I was just dying. And drinking. And a person can't keep that up forever. It wasn't long before the gig was up and it all came crumbling down.

When that happened, I knew my public image was about to collapse. I felt everything was hanging on by a little thread. But you know what? When it did collapse, when everything was at its most painful, that pain became the touchstone of my spiritual growth, emotional growth, and transformation.

It takes courage to admit we need to let go. It was hard for me to do that, but not as hard as trying to hold it all together to maintain the illusion of my supposed well-managed life. (That was a far cry from seeking all the help I really needed.)

I believe that when we're honest with ourselves, we feel this power within. I think it comes from a quiet sense and an inner knowing. When we listen to ourselves, we develop the power of choice. We get to be in the driver's seat and take actionable steps in the right direction.

It's the moment when we step into the side of ourselves that realizes change is possible, hope is available, and that there is a solution.

Actionable Steps

Practice mindfulness. Engage in activities that bring your focus to the present, such as deep breathing exercises, meditation, or simply paying attention to your surroundings.

Practice letting go. Acknowledge your thoughts about the past or future, then gently redirect your focus back to the present moment. Accept what you cannot change and focus on what you can control now.

Engage fully in activities. Whether you're working, spending time with loved ones, or enjoying a hobby, fully immerse yourself in the experience. No distractions, no multitasking. Establish "no phone times"—especially during dinner—and put your tech away. When I am on a job I do my best to be 100% all in and focused on performing. When I am at home, I do my best to put my phone down when my daughter is talking to me and also do my best to answer emails only when I am in my home office working.

Cultivate gratitude in the moment. Take moments throughout your day to appreciate the little things in life: a beautiful sunset, a warm cup of tea, or a kind gesture from someone. Make this practice even more impactful by writing down what you're thankful for, sharing it, and listening to what someone else is grateful for.

Practice acceptance. Embrace the life unfolding before you, moment by moment. Let go of the urge to constantly strive for something different. Acceptance enables us to find contentment and peace in *this* moment.

Key Takeaway

We heal what we reveal. You are powerful beyond measure.

6

The Art of Letting Go

Releasing the Past to Embrace a Brighter Future

You know that old saying about getting back on the horse? Well, after my motorcycle accident, my horse was my career as a physical fitness trainer. I clung to that horse through my 34 surgeries and all the painful, slow healing that followed them, spending hours and hours focusing on how I could get back to training clients.

You could say I got a little caught up in it.

When I was bedridden in the hospital, I worked on training plans for my clients and spoke to them over the phone when I could. And then one glorious day, I was finally able to come home. I was still months away from being able to climb the stairs to my bedroom—heck, using a real toilet instead of a bed-pan loomed on a distant horizon—but I was inside the four walls of my house. Never mind that I had a hospital bed set up in the living room. Never mind that I couldn't yet stand for more than a few moments at a time, let alone go to the gym. I was home.

Back to work, I resolved, *in whatever way I can.*

When I could manage crutches, I started training one of my clients, Debbie, at my house. The pain was so bad when I first started—bad enough that I had to excuse myself from our session one morning so I could hobble to the bathroom on my crutches and throw up. Some people might have canceled the remainder of the session right then and there, but that's not me. I sure did go right back out to the living room and finish Debbie's session.

In hindsight, the fact that Debbie kept me on as her trainer in those early days seems like it was more for me than for her. (I tell her that sometimes. We live states apart now, but I still train her over Zoom. She disagrees, of course, because she's so wonderful.) Either way, her choice enabled me to continue the pursuit of what I thought was my purpose during a critical period in my life.

Despite the fact that I was healing, and despite the fact I'd continued to work through my recovery, my confidence was shaky. *I'm broken*, I thought. *Who's going to want to train with me?*

Eventually I was cleared to go back to work in earnest, and the first thing I did was to start calling more of my clients. "Hey, I'm back," I would say, doubt still circling with every phone call. "I can start training you again."

To my surprise, my training business *boomed*.

People had seen me at the gym, working out in a wheelchair, on crutches, with a walker, and then back in a wheelchair. I can't tell you how often someone approached me during that period of my life to tell me that they hadn't felt like working out that day, but then they'd seen me—with all the restraints and limitations my accident had placed on my physical body—working out no matter what. Most thought if I could do it despite my wheelchair, they could do it despite their attitude. And they did.

The good and bad news was that I got busy *fast*. It was good news for all the obvious career-building reasons. It was bad news because my pain intensified to a near-breaking point. Because I refused to let go of my career, I was, quite literally, killing myself.

It all came to a head one day when Johnny and I were at the gym together. I was wearing one of those medical boots, and inside it my stitches had come open. To say I was *merely bleeding* is an understatement. But I did what I do and continued training my client.

Suddenly Johnny stopped me, his face pale with shock.

"Amberly, what are you *doing*?" he demanded. "There is a *trail of blood* following you around the gym. You're bleeding out."

That's what it took for me to realize my old career wasn't working for me anymore.

The truth hit me hard. I wasn't serving my clients to the best standard. I wasn't serving my family, and I certainly wasn't serving myself. *Something has to change*, I thought. *I can't do this anymore—I have to figure out something else.*

The realization was profoundly convincing, but accepting that reality was still hard. The temptation to see it as "accepting defeat," or admitting I'd been wrong in some devastating way, loomed large. I had to work through that and reframe it. Yes, one career was ending. But I needed to acknowledge the whole reality: I wasn't admitting defeat. I was acknowledging that it was time for me to take better care of myself and my family.

The truth I came to realize was this. If I continued clinging to the past—if I continued trying to fix what was broken—I would get stuck there. I've never been one for getting stuck, not even when confined to that hospital bed, so I needed to look ahead and imagine what I might create with what was new.

Looking back on those days of struggling through training clients, it's easy to see how my current career was waiting for me the whole time to discover it. There I'd be, on the bike at the gym, doing the only cardio I was physically able to do after my accident. Person after person after person would come up to me for advice. They'd tell me their problems. Ask me if I could call their struggling aunt. At one point, someone noticed what was happening. "Oh my gosh, Amberly," they said. "Doesn't that drive you crazy?"

"Well, no," I answered. "It makes me feel good because I know I can help them."

Peppered in with the people asking for advice were those who encouraged me to tell my story. "You could really inspire people," they insisted.

Something clicked.

I have always loved being able to connect with people and offer any kind of guidance and support that I can. Back when I was in the hospital after my motorcycle accident, there was always a chair in the corner of my room. Nurses would come in, plop themselves down, and ask me for advice. That has always come easily for me.

Too often, when something comes really easy for us, we discount it. Maybe we just don't recognize it. But pay attention to those things that come easily. More often than not, they're connected to your purpose.

Me, I knew I wanted to affect people on a larger scale. Sharing my story with someone at the gym was great and all, but how could I help more than one person at a time?

Well, I thought, *that might be an idea*. And suddenly, there it was: a new thing I could imagine and create.

It took letting go of my fitness career to realize I could make that bigger impact.

Through speaking and writing.

Outcome, I Release You

That's not to say I sailed off into the sunset and smoothly arrived at success. Plain and simple, it was a lot of trial and error and learning what worked and what didn't.

A lot of what worked was letting go, over and over again.

Eventually I was asked to speak at a networking event that catered to lawyers, realtors, and financial advisors. And I realized . . . I didn't even own a suit.

So I found myself at Nordstrom—on my way to speak, no less—telling a sales associate I only really owned workout clothes but needed to buy a suit. She asked me about my size and tastes. She was good at her job. Would I be good at this?

In fact, the whole time I was there I was thinking, *What am I doing? Why am I going to speak to all these smart, successful people? Why would any of them want to listen to me?* I remember calling my dad and telling him what I was doing. If I was looking for an "atta girl, go get 'em" . . . well.

"Why in the heck would you ever do that?" Dad practically shouted through the phone. "Don't you know that public speaking is the number one fear of most people in the world other than death?"

Thanks, Dad.

"Well," he continued, "just remember one thing. This isn't about you. This is about the people you serve."

Dad's words were a masterclass in shifting my perspective, and I carry them with me today. I still get intimidated, but when

I focus on helping the people I'm there to serve, it takes all the nerves out of the equation because it helps me let go of any outcome for myself.

Letting go is so many things. Letting go of an outcome is what really enables you to do your best. You can—and should—prepare as much as you can, but then know God's got the rest. But letting go is *also* knowing that you're going to have challenging times. You're going to have failures. For me, that makes letting go all about releasing shame and anything else that is no longer serving me.

Just like success, letting go doesn't necessarily come easy. First, you have to acknowledge that mistakes happen and failure is just a natural part of growth and learning. Then you have to make a practice of learning something from every single experience. Past experience is our most powerful teacher.

A few years back, I spoke to 350 members of the California Professional Firefighters association. My audience was packed with captains and high-level firefighters.

Just imagine walking into a room full of tough guys with handlebar mustaches and tattoos to give a talk about emotional resilience. I was tasked with giving that particular keynote—and a question-and-answer (Q&A) session afterwards—to an audience of people who didn't want to admit they were emotional or talk about things that were hard.

Unsurprisingly, not a single person raised their hand during my Q&A.

Well, I thought, *this has never happened before.*

Afterward, Johnny explained to me that appearing weak or vulnerable could be a career killer for groups like firefighters and cops. Alright, that's fair. I still didn't want the awkward silence that filled my Q&A session to ever happen to me again. So, when I went to speak at Google, I brought five copies of my book to the Q&A and offered them for free to the first five people who raised their hand.

See, I couldn't control what would happen at Google, and I let go of trying. But that doesn't mean I didn't take steps to *prepare* for the outcome I wanted. Those two things are not mutually exclusive. Turns out I'm not afraid to bribe people to get the ball rolling—and it worked. As soon as I offered my book, hands shot up all over the room.

Reflection: The Kindness of Letting Go

Learning from our experiences and using the knowledge to improve our future, learning to speak to ourselves with the same kindness we would have for someone that we love—those are the things you just can't get until you let go of whatever is holding you back.

Remember, acceptance is the first step toward letting go. You can't let go of something if you haven't acknowledged and accepted it exists.

That was a hard lesson for me to learn. After my motorcycle accident—after I'd endured so many surgeries and treatments—I was in so much pain that I thought having my leg amputated was the solution. But that was because I didn't want to accept the pain. I didn't want to accept the way my leg looked. I was still hiding all my scars from the world.

I remember an incredibly hot day in California around that time. I was wearing shorts, but insisted on wearing knee-high boots. My girlfriend couldn't believe it, but when she asked me about it I doubled down. "I'm never going to show my scars," I vowed. "No one's ever going to see these."

At the root of it, I was trying to hide the fact that something was wrong with me. I was unwilling to accept that new reality, and I was willing to *have my leg cut off* rather than acknowledge and accept the pain. That last resort—that fate I'd been fighting to avoid—I opened my arms to it. Had my doctor not intervened by calling my leg a work of art, had I not found a way to accept and let go, my life today would be very, very different. I might not be writing this book; you might not be reading it.

Acceptance literally changed my life.

When you're in acceptance and can shine a light on your pain, your shame, or your mistakes, it completely dissolves that pain. That's what makes it your superpower.

It is a kindness.

To you.

When I was preparing to do my TED Talk, I got so anxious. I would literally sit up late at night, paralyzed by the loop of my thoughts: *Oh my gosh, oh my gosh, I only have two weeks until I'm going this talk in front of thousands of people, oh my gosh, oh my gosh . . .*

It happened a lot. But every time I got that way, I would stop what I was doing, go upstairs, and go practice my talk. Just taking that one actionable step jolted me out of the worry loop and alleviated the fear and anxiety I felt.

It also helped me be kinder to myself.

At its core, letting go is really just practicing self-compassion. It is realizing we all make mistakes and then treating ourselves with kindness. I've already said I would never verbally (or physically, for that matter) beat someone up for missing a deadline, forgetting an assignment, or just generally messing up. You probably wouldn't, either. Why is it that we so often do that to ourselves?

Letting go tames that inner critic—that bully who lives in our heads—and teaches us to be a little kinder to ourselves. Admittedly, that can be easy to know and hard to do. What really helps us let go of the past is being fully in the present moment.

Why is that? Well, a lot of times when we're in the past we're caught up in coming down on ourselves for things we can't change, which can lead to depression. However, constantly being in the future—usually by worrying about it in some way, shape, or form—can cause anxiety.

Focusing on the present by setting realistic goals and taking actionable steps toward them can keep us grounded. Personally, it keeps me from becoming overwhelmed with big, looming tasks and accidentally letting that inner bully out of jail. Taking just *one* actionable step gets me in the present moment and helps me feel I'm moving in the right direction.

If I had to guess, I'd say most of us who identify as "overcoming perfectionists" have had an experience like that. We know those moments of freaking out really cost us time and energy that we need to be able to do our lives. But it's so easy to get frozen in fear. It happens to me all the time. A lot of people are surprised by that, but it's true.

But treating ourselves with more kindness means not allowing that fear to rob us of our joy.

See, there are things we can learn from our fears and anxieties. The day before I gave my talk at Google, I told Johnny I was already *really* nervous. "You always get nervous," he reminded me. "That's part of you. It'd be weird if you didn't get that way. It means you care."

He was right—and he helped me reframe the anxiety I felt into a kindness. Now I can see it for what it is: a reminder of how much I care about the people I serve.

It's easier to let go of an outcome when we practice that particular self-kindness and replace negative, self-critical thoughts with more positive and constructive ones. Me, I remind myself of my strengths. I remind myself of my past successes. I remember a client who took me to the side before I gave my TED Talk—when I was stuck in reminding myself that I was the only speaker who didn't have a PhD, who didn't even go to college, and why would anyone want to hear what I had to say—and reminded me of that I was *not* less than. I was strong and capable.

"Amberly," she said, "you made it through 34 surgeries. You can get on that stage and stand there and talk."

"Okay," I said. "You're right. I can do this."

And I did.

Actionable Steps

Acknowledge and accept your feelings. Allow yourself to acknowledge any emotions tied to past experiences. Recognize that it's normal to feel these emotions, but don't let them define or dictate your future.

Visualize letting go. When we can visualize ourselves letting go of the past and moving forward with confidence, we're much more able to actually do it. Visualization works in all sorts of scenarios—whether it's stepping out onstage and imagining doing a good job, or starting a business and having a ton of new clients, when we visualize it, we do it. Heck, I did it when I was a kid without even realizing it. If I could visualize myself doing three perfect pirouettes in the dance studio, I could actually do them. If I couldn't visualize it, I couldn't do it. Seeing it in my head made the difference.

Practice forgiveness. Forgive yourself and others for past mistakes or hurtful actions.

Focus on the present and the future. Shift your attention away from dwelling on past events. Instead, focus on the opportunities and possibilities that lie ahead. Set new goals, pursue new interests, and invest your energy in creating a fulfilling future for yourself.

Key Takeaway

Change is hard, but being flexible and open to new opportunities is life-changing. Let go of what is no longer serving you and embrace the brightness ahead.

CHAPTER

7

Discovering Your Joy
A Blueprint for Uncovering Personal Passions and Pursuits That Ignite Happiness

You know by now that public speaking always makes me nervous. But I do it again and again because of the feedback I get from people who come up to me after an event to tell me that something I shared about my life changed theirs. Maybe something shifted their perspective; maybe they even decided to get sober. But it brings me so much joy to get to connect with attendees after I walk off stage.

When I spoke at Google, a woman approached me and started to cry. "I could just feel the love and the light just pouring out of you," she said. "I could see how much you really care."

She was right—I care, and I care a lot. And when I can make an impact, it's so fulfilling. I love knowing I can be in service to others and help them with their success.

I've always been an encourager. I see someone who's struggling and I want to go over and help them or encourage them and lift them up. I want to show them in some way that I believe in them—and that they can believe in themselves. Encouraging people has always come so naturally to me. I can easily focus on a solution, or be flexible in finding a new one if the solution a person has isn't really working for them.

All that to say, the fact that I could encourage people in their business, their fitness, and their relationships has always been right there in my face. It comes easily and it really fuels me and brings me joy—especially in my Mastermind group. The fact that I have so many women I get to encourage, that I get to see one woman go from having no confidence to having a best-selling book and doing her own podcasts and speaking on media platforms is incredible. When I can help someone and see them start to transform their lives physically, mentally, and emotionally—wow! It lights me up.

Like I mentioned in Chapter 6, I came to public speaking as a result of constant comments from others that nudged me in the direction of public speaking. Still, there is a moment that sticks out in my memory as the one I began to think about my love for helping others as a career.

I had already begun giving talks, and I was sitting in my office prepping for the next one on my schedule. It was a big one—I was to speak in front of hundreds of people. The closer it got, the more nervous I became. Like I used to do while running track, I started talking to God.

"Oh, my goodness," I said, "this is hard. God, I just don't think I'm cut out for this. It's too scary. It's *too* hard."

My phone rang.

"Amberly," the person on the other end of the line said, "I'm doing an event and we're expecting a few thousand people. I'd love for you to speak."

There I was, sweating it out over speaking to 300 people, and a request comes in to speak to 3,000. *Okay, God,* I thought, *you've got a pretty good sense of humor.*

I accepted.

Fast-forward a few years, to the event at Google. When they approached me about giving a talk, I was knee-deep in working on this book. *Oh my goodness,* I thought, *I have so much going on. I need to be working on my book. I need to be getting my annual UNSTOPPABLE Success Summit event together. I really don't want to fly across the country.*

I ended up giving that talk all the same.

It can be easy to come up with excuses when we're intimidated, or busy, or overwhelmed. But if I'm being honest, I've never regretted taking a single booking. Why would I when I'm so passionate about helping people? When what I do lights me up inside?

Discovering Your Purpose . . . for Now

Helping others through speaking, podcasting, and coaching is my purpose. It fuels me and ignites my happiness. It's also something I never dreamed of back in my days as a professional dancer. So how did I get here?

Yes, all those people who encouraged me in this direction were instrumental in getting me here. But before all that, there came a point in my dance career when I was ready to retire from dancing.

In the years leading up to my 25th birthday, I'd been making trips to Japan twice a year to dance. The job paid well, and I enjoyed it. But age 25 is often considered old for a dancer, and I'd always had it in my mind that when I hit that mark I wasn't going to do it anymore.

But by the time I reached that so-called dance retirement age, I was also a single mom. I needed the money I earned in Japan. The last time I went, though, my daughter turned a year old while I was away—and it absolutely crushed me that I wasn't with her.

Dance had always felt like my passion. My purpose. What I was put on this planet to do. But on that trip, something was different. I didn't want to do what I was doing. I didn't want to travel, or be on a set for long periods of time.

I've got to do something else, I thought. And the question I asked myself in that moment was simple: what brings me joy?

I'd been teaching dance since I was 13—had I ever stopped to ask that question? But I knew, without a doubt, that what brought me joy was working with people. I also knew I loved working out and moving my body. I had even gone to the gym and worked through a knee injury that my doctor wanted to do surgery on—I rehabbed that knee myself, through fitness, and was able to cancel my surgery.

If I can do this for me, I thought, *I can help others this way, too.*

I started exploring what careers would enable me to help people the way I'd helped myself. My first thought was *physical therapist*, but the cost of school and the investment of time it would require were both too high. I ruled it out.

Personal training, however, felt like a good fit. So I went out and got certified as a personal trainer while I kept up with a waitressing gig on the side—which I hated, by the way—until I could build up my clientele. But the process of discovering my passion led me to take a bold step and quit my waitressing job before I had a solid client base. In effect, I gave myself a really productive pain point. I had bills to pay, and now—no way to pay them. *I better get some clients quick*, I thought.

I did. And I also quickly realized how much I loved training clients. Soon it became my (new) purpose and passion.

See, I've changed careers three times in my life. I went from a professional dancer to personal trainer to coach, speaker, and podcaster. And I think it's really important to acknowledge those changes, because so many times we're told that we're supposed to have one passion and purpose in life.

But what's been true in my life is something else entirely, and it's led me to believe that we *don't* have to have a single purpose to carry us through the rest of our lives. It's okay if our focus changes and we realize there's something else we want to do.

Reflection: Dreaming Just Won't Get You There

We live in a world full of aspirational images, videos, media, careers . . . from the outside looking in, it can seem like there's a yawning gulf between a person and the gorgeous, accomplished person they see on a screen. *Oh wow, they've got it easy*, we think. *Everything comes naturally for them.*

But isn't that an incredibly discouraging way to see the world? I think so. That's why I spend so much time telling people who have seen videos of me working out, or onstage dancing, or about to give a keynote that I did not wake up one morning and find myself in this life.

In fact, I spent six years recovering after my motorcycle accident before I ever started sharing anything about it. I was sober for an entire year before I even told people I was taking it one day at a time, and years before I even said anything about my sobriety on social media.

And I never would've gotten here if I hadn't set goals for myself along the way.

When I was stuck in that hospital bed, just about anyone and everyone told me I would never walk again. *Oh, I'm going to walk*, I thought.

Well, I couldn't even stand up. I was completely, utterly bedridden. In fact, at the time, I couldn't even lift my leg off the hospital bed when the physical therapist came to visit me five days a week at my home. There was a brief moment when I did wonder, *Am I paralyzed on one side?*

I was determined. I visualized myself being able to move my leg again. Each time my therapist came over I looked down at my leg and willed it to move. I know that might seem kind of crazy, but it eventually worked and I could miraculously lift my leg up a couple of inches.

Eventually I did get out of bed. I did stand—for mere seconds at a time. But it was painful—so painful. I wasn't even putting pressure on my injury, but the blood rushing to it was excruciating enough to make me almost pass out.

But each day when the physical therapist showed up, I would tell myself, *I'm going to make sure I can stand up for 10 seconds.*

Ten seconds.

Talk about breaking down a goal into small steps. But if I'd gone straight to thinking about running another marathon, it would've just been this big idea. I would've been discouraged because it was so unattainable. But 10 seconds? I could do that. I could survive the pain for that long.

Soon my 10 seconds became 20.

Then 30.

A minute.

Five minutes.

The day I was able to stand long enough—with crutches—that I could make it around the corner to the bathroom and not have to use a bed pan? All those 10-second small goals added up to a huge victory. By the way, my first goal was to be able to lift my leg, second to stand with crutches for 10 seconds, because I knew these things would get me to my main goal at the time—being able to use the bathroom on my own without that dang bedpan.

That's how small goals snowball into bigger ones.

Every small victory builds confidence and makes it easier to take on the next challenge. And that's what you need to do if you want to live your dreams.

Hear me loud and clear on this: having *ideas* about what you want to do is not the same as having *goals* that will get you there. Ideas can stay in your head—you can have one without taking any action at all.

Having a goal is different.

From time to time, I have to give one of my Mastermind students a come-to-Jesus talk about this. They'll join my group with the idea that they want to start a podcast, or host an online course, and I give them all the suggestions and connections in my arsenal to help them along. But all they do is continue dreaming.

Dreams are wonderful, and we need them. But when you have a dream without setting a goal—or when you go through life without setting specific, achievable goals related to your interests and passions—those dreams stay dreams. They're never going to become reality.

If you want that to change, you have to set your big goals, break them down into smaller steps so you can create a plan, and work toward attaining them.

That's how you start living your passions.

Actionable Steps

Set goals and break them down into small, achievable steps. Don't think you'll go from "can't walk" to "marathon superstar" on a dream. Stay consistent, but don't forget to be open-minded and take care of yourself along the way.

Keep persisting, but make it a point to adapt instead of giving up when things get hard. Starting a business is hard in a lot of ways, but it can be especially hard during the years you're only breaking even. It took several years before I really started making money as a speaker, but each year gets better. If I would have stopped during the break-even years, I wouldn't be where I am today.

Dedicate time for reflection. If we want to find those new things, some self-reflection and exploration is an absolute must. Take the time to reflect on your interests, values, and strengths. What activities make you feel energized and engaged? What are you passionate about? What do you value most in life?

Think of it this way. If I were someone who hated working out and would rather be a couch potato and watch Netflix than go on a run, my purpose probably *wouldn't* have been to become a fitness trainer. But running was my drug of choice and always had been. My love for working out easily translated into geeking out on biomechanics, human anatomy, and the Krebs cycle. Turned out, I loved learning about how our energy is processed. I was obsessed with assessing the way another person walked, realizing what caused this hitch or that tightness, and knowing which stretch or exercise would help them improve their gait. Heck, even when I was in the hospital with my leg completely open all the way down to the bone,

I was fascinated by the fact that I could see all the striations in my muscles. Most people wouldn't even look at that. I couldn't look away.

All that was a natural bridge to teaching others to do the same.

I'm not suggesting very many people want to compare what's under their own skin with an anatomy textbook, but I am saying you have to know what lights you up inside. If you don't, it's important to get out there and explore different activities. Try new things, interests, career paths. Pay attention to how each activity makes you feel. Do you feel energized when you think about starting it? Or do you feel drained and try to procrastinate? Does it align with your values?

And that's the trick. Pay attention to what sparks your joy, but pay equal attention to what your natural inclination is—and then let those things line up.

Find what—and who—inspires you and immerse yourself. It's so important to surround yourself with people who inspire you and share your interests and passions. That's what a lot of people don't understand about the industry I'm in right now. Everybody wants to be a speaker. Everybody wants to be an author. Everybody wants to know how I'm getting so many speaking events, guest spots on other podcasts, and big-name guests on my own.

Here's the secret: I attend events. I seek out people on social media who really inspire me, follow them, and read their books. I listen to their podcasts. I don't do it because I'm trying to get a guest spot or an interview. I do it because these individuals really, truly inspire me to keep up my own work. I want their voices in my life for that reason alone. And I want to build relationships with them whenever I can because I deeply admire them.

For the record, I don't follow people just for follow-backs. I don't follow accounts just because one follows me. In the beginning of my social media journey, I would feel like I needed to follow people back if they followed me, so I did. But now I don't unless they really inspire me or I really feel like they're authentic. And wow, when you lock into your own authenticity and values—when you start to really know what your beliefs are and what's important to you—it's crazy how you start to attract others who share the same ones.

It's also crazy how the money follows.

Challenge yourself. Stepping out of your comfort zone, taking on new challenges, and really pushing yourself to try new things and overcome obstacles is another must. Growth comes from facing your challenges and pushing past your limitations—it's just that simple. Each time you do something, it builds that confidence muscle. You learn that you can do something hard because *you've already accomplished hard things.*

Before I walked onstage at Google, when my nerves were coming for me, I didn't even care that the room I was speaking in didn't have a backstage area. I walked to an area where some ladies were standing.

"Excuse me," I said, "I just need to do some real quick push-ups." Then I dropped to the floor in my dress and boots, did my push-ups, and hopped back up to walk up onstage.

Why? Because push-ups are hard, and doing them boosts my confidence. Successfully meeting that challenge helps me tackle the next one in front of me. That's just one strategy I have for managing my feelings when I get scared. Sometimes, before I'm about to do something that scares me, I ask myself,

"What's a hard thing I've overcome?" Well, as I mentioned in Chapter 6, I overcame 34 surgeries. I can surely get onstage and talk.

Key Takeaway

Sometimes our purpose is right in front of us and we don't realize it because it comes so easily.

8

Building Meaningful Connections

Nurturing Relationships That Foster Joy

Have you ever heard of an energy vampire? They're exactly what they sound like: people who completely drain your emotional and physical energy with their constant complaining, excessive negativity, or demanding attention (and sometimes with all three). Any interaction with them—whether over the phone, on Zoom, or in social media—leaves you exhausted and depleted. Personally, I think being on Zoom with an energy vampire is the absolute worst. It feels like being held hostage.

Tell an energy vampire anything good that's going on in your life and they'll put a damper on it. They'll shut it down; they'll tell you why it isn't going to work. For instance, you could tell them you've won the lottery. They'll just remind you that you're going to have to pay taxes on all those winnings.

Like all of us, I learned about energy vampires through personal experience. After I was diagnosed with complex regional pain syndrome (CRPS), I was determined to find a community or support group. At the time, I was pretty new to Facebook, but I thought, *Maybe I could search for other people who've been diagnosed with this condition and find my people. My CRPS people. We could support each other and lean on each other.* In the face of my frightening, unyielding diagnosis, that hope was a beacon.

Well, I found a group. And I went in like I always do, looking at the upside of things and being as positive as I could.

It wasn't long before I noticed that I was the only one doing that.

In fact, it's not a stretch to say everyone else in that particular group was just so *negative.* All they did was complain, show pictures of their flare-ups, and generally try to outdo each other's hurts. "The treatment doesn't work," they'd write. "You're never going to get a cure."

I pressed forward, as I do. Meanwhile, I was asked to be a guest on the television show *The Doctors.* On the day of filming, the doctors themselves interviewed me for a long, long time. I felt it had gone well. But TV being what TV is, they promptly cut down my interview to isolate one particular part of the conversation.

See, during taping I'd discussed all the alternative methods for combating the CRPS that I'd tried: ketamine, a spinal block, a spinal stimulator, Eastern and Western medicine. At one point I was on 73 homeopathic pills a day and 11 prescription medications. Do you think any of that made it to air? Nope. It was all left behind on the editors' chopping block.

Well, what did make it to air was about to kick my ass.

I spoke about how none of those methods worked for me—not the medicines, not the spinal interventions, not the ketamine.

"Fighting CRPS pain began with my mindset," I said. "I learned I had to work on myself mentally, physically, and spiritually if I wanted to have the life I'd always imagined."

I shared that along with my PACER method, which I'll share with you in Chapter 13, and then I went through my whole method for shifting perspective, being in acceptance, being in the right community, having endurance, being persistent, and the importance of rest. All of it. But do you think that was the headline for the episode?

I wish it had been, but no.

It was not.

The headline that *did* accompany my episode was something along the lines of "Woman Gets Through Pain with Mindset."

Let me tell you, the haters came out of the woodwork.

And they came with the most force from my CRPS group.

Listen—I thought that group was my community. My *people*. But there I was, phone blowing up with criticism and beratement. To be fair, several people in the group—the ones who actually knew me—were taking up for me. Everyone else basically said, "That author is full of crap."

It was unequivocally horrible, and it didn't stop there.

"There's no way she even has CRPS," the haters said, my phone pinging nonstop with notifications. "How could she? You can't get through this pain with mindset."

For a while, I would get in there and read all the hate they were spewing at me. The onslaught included general internet nastiness, but it still stung. Exhibit A: "If she had CRPS, she couldn't wear those shoes." Again with the shoes?! They didn't know that I'd worn my comfy boots—the only shoes I could really wear—that entire day, and had only changed into pretty shoes right before I stepped onstage. Heaven help me for wanting to look nice on national television. Heaven help me for wanting to sit down in a chair not wearing my barn boots with a nice dress.

It was just *crazy.*

And it was sucking the life out of me.

No Is Enough

Not long after that CRPS group came for me like the villagers raiding the castle at the end of *Beauty and the Beast*, I was about to go onstage to speak at a conference for women empowering women.

Listen, women empowering women is my thing. It is a *huge* part of why I do what I do. So I should have been elated that day, but instead I remember sitting in the makeup chair with tears rolling down my face. I couldn't believe the outpouring of negativity from the CRPS group. I felt so hurt, so betrayed, and it was really affecting me.

Then, out of nowhere, a thought crept in.

I'm outta here.

No, I didn't bail on the conference. But I sure did turn off the notifications and leave that toxic group. *I don't want to hear it,* I thought. Because the truth was, those people were not actually my people—not in the way I'd hoped they would be. Once I accepted that, the solution was right there. I could simply say no.

It sounds so simple, doesn't it? Well, that's because it is. In that moment, the recognition enabled me to pause, take a breath, and think, *Wait a minute. I really can set this boundary. I have the power to do that.*

The solution was more than just blocking notifications, and it's not lost on me that I empowered myself to set that boundary right before heading out onstage to empower other women.

But I decided right then and there that in place of those relationships with the energy vampires in my life, I could foster ones that bring me joy. And it all started with a simple no.

Me, I had to learn that it could be that simple. I had to learn that *no* is one of the most powerful words we have. And I also had to learn that I could also say no *without giving an explanation*.

Let that one settle in.

Look—there's a lot of social conditioning we women experience that says we don't have that power. There's been a stink in the air for generations that says we should always, *always* explain ourselves. Well, I'm saying no to that, too.

You don't have to explain why you can't do something.

You don't have to explain why you can't talk on the phone.

And I don't have to spend a paragraph in an email explaining why I couldn't do this interview or that collaboration.

No can be a sentence. It's all that's needed. *No* is enough.

Different Strokes for Different Folks

I say this a lot, but it bears repeating. When it comes to the energy vampires in your life, sometimes you've got to bless 'em and block 'em.

That said, different relationships mean we set boundaries differently. It was one thing for me to set boundaries in relationships with an online support group full of people I didn't know well. When it came down to it, I left that Facebook group pretty easily. Setting boundaries with a friend or family member is something else entirely.

Simply put, it's harder.

There might be events or holidays or work-related things at which you'll have to see the person. We can't avoid everyone forever. You need a new strategy to stave off the energy vampires in your life whom you have to see.

That's when setting healthy boundaries for how much time you're willing to spend with them—and what physical spaces you'll allow them into—becomes really important.

I had a friend who constantly wanted to get together while I was writing my first book. We'll call her Shayla. Shayla was in the middle of her own big project at the same time I was writing my book, and I thought working on these projects side-by-side would give us something constructive to talk about.

Boy, was I wrong.

Every time we got together, all Shayla wanted to do was complain—about politics, about how awful the world was, about how she couldn't find the right man or the right job or the right kind of ice cream. It was relentless. Even worse, she wouldn't do anything to change her circumstances and she was not open to suggestions.

As you can probably imagine, my desire to spend time with her dwindled into nothing. I had a full-time job, a family at home, and demanding side projects to boot. But even though Shayla reliably sucked the life out of me when I made time to meet her for dinner, I was having a hard time refusing her constant invitations. Saying no might be simple, but that doesn't always make it easy.

Even when I made my excuses, she still wanted to get together.

I managed to put her off for a while, but finally I agreed to meet her. *She's been asking forever to go to dinner*, I thought. *So I'll go out to dinner*.

I decided the healthy thing to do was decide in advance how much time I was willing to endure her complaining. *An hour and a half*, I promised myself, and away I went.

The dinner was every bit as negative as I'd feared it would be. "Hey," I said after 90 minutes had elapsed, "I've got to get going."

"No," she said. "This hasn't been enough time with you. I need more."

It's never going to be enough, I thought, *because you're an energy vampire and you depend on someone like me for your own energy. You want to suck the energy out of me because you don't have any.*

I didn't say that to her, of course. But that was the last time I went to dinner with her, all the same.

Did I ever regret that decision? No. And every time her name popped up on my phone, it confirmed that I'd done the right thing. When somebody's an energy vampire, you know it when you see their name come up on your phone. *Oh man*, you think. *Oh man, not this person again. What do they want now?*

I always say that in a world of energy vampires, you've got to stick with the puppy uppers and get rid of the doggy downers. When you see names pop up on your phone and feel excited, stick with those people. They'll spark joy in your life instead of snuffing it out.

But if you absolutely must see a person who is an energy vampire, choosing the right venue for the meeting is also really important. It was no accident that I met Shayla for dinner outside my home. I'd already learned not to let her come to my house.

Because the last time she was there, I could not get her to leave. Finally, Johnny, Ruby, and I were all walking out the door to get to an appointment.

"We have to go," I said.

"Oh, but I just wanted to show you more of my project," she replied.

I didn't let her come over to my house anymore after that. Every time she wanted to get together, I thought, *No, no, no. I'll meet you at a restaurant.*

Fallout Can Happen

Back when I was doing in-home personal training, I had a wealthy client with so much negative energy that I had to visualize protective armor around myself every time I interacted with her. She and her husband fought all the time, and one day when I went to train her, I walked into her house to the sound of breaking glass. Yes, she was actually picking up things around the house and throwing them against the wall.

I can't be around this negativity and anger anymore, I thought. It was awful to be in proximity to that, so I gathered my courage and spoke to her. "I'm so sorry," I said, "but I won't be able to train you anymore."

I think nobody had ever said no to her—at least not for a very long time—until I did that day.

"I'll pay you more," was her first response. "What do you want—$200 an hour? I'll pay you $300 an hour."

"I'm sorry, but no," I said again. "This isn't about the money."

See, I knew it was about my mental, physical, and emotional health. I couldn't put a dollar amount on that, so I couldn't be around her. Well, she kept calling me and calling me. I'll never forget seeing her name pop up on my phone when Johnny and I were at dinner one evening before we got married. I looked at him and he looked at me.

"Don't even listen to that message," he said. "It's not going to be good. Just delete it."

He really helped me that day. I followed his advice, and that meant she didn't get free rent in my head. I blocked her number and never heard from her again.

But that doesn't mean any of it was easy.

Another time, I had to set boundaries with a friend I had before my business started to pick up. About the same time I was on *The Today Show* and my first book had become a best-seller, all this friend wanted to do was go to a ladies' lunch to sit and complain.

Unlike I'd felt with Shayla, I wanted to see this friend, but her negativity didn't fuel my joy at all. I needed to be around someone with a growth mindset—someone who had big ideas about changing the world for the better. This friend was disgruntled any time I said I couldn't meet her (heck, I had plenty of days during that period of my life that I was so busy I forgot to eat lunch), and eventually our friendship ran its course. We grew apart.

It wasn't easy. It was sad. We'd been very close for a long time. But I eventually realized the distance between us is better.

When you set boundaries, fallout can and will happen. That's as it should be (even though it's difficult and sad). But in the long run, it's always easier to say no up-front than it is to spend your time in a way you'll resent later. Because that's the way it works. Every time you say yes to something, you're saying no to something else. Every time I say yes to something, I'm saying no to my family. I'm saying no to my workouts. I'm saying no to the things that I need to do to build my business.

Think through what you're saying no to when you say yes to something else. Then, use that information to help you set your boundaries. Prioritize what's important to you. And remember— you're not being selfish when you say no to something. Those right relationships in your life—with the people who will always have your back, no matter what—will understand and support your choices.

And those right relationships will pull you forward.

With a Little Help from My Friend

Some of the ladies in my Mastermind group have some real trauma they're working through. Me being me, I want to be in the trenches with every single one of them as they're on the road to recovery. But supporting someone looks different than that at times. For instance, sometimes support is helping a friend or colleague set boundaries.

I was lucky enough to experience that at my recent annual event when another speaker came and took me to the side and gave me the business.

"Amberly," she said, "you are really going to have to set some boundaries. You're going to have to keep that Bible close to you and make sure everyone is not texting and calling you all the time. They'll suck your energy."

This speaker is very intuitive, and she really helped me learn to prioritize my own positivity. If I didn't set the boundaries for myself, she indicated, someone else would set them for me with their negativity.

I want to be around people who are the victors of their own lives, not ones who cling to a victim mindset.

And look—sometimes we need help with that.

When I'm hosting an event, sometimes it's harder for me to set and maintain boundaries because I'm there to support people and I want to be there to listen. But I literally can't even go to the bathroom without attendees following me in and talking to me while I'm in a stall.

Well, at this same recent event, I had an event planner for the first time. This woman was a godsend. She was like my bodyguard, directing traffic away from me or pulling me out of conversations with a simple, "We need Amberly over here, please." She even escorted me to the green room so I could get organized, change clothes, and come back out again. I call her my gatekeeper—and I really believe we all need gatekeepers in our life.

"I know you're not feeling great," she said to me as I was about to attend the event lunch, "so you're going to go in your room and I'm going to bring you food. Lay down and kick your leg up until I get there."

I did as she asked, and you know something? I needed her to help me set that boundary to promote my own energy and well-being. I wanted to talk with every last person there who wanted to talk with me, but when I do that I walk away completely drained because I don't get any downtime to recover. My planner helped me set that boundary so I could conserve my energy and use it when it mattered the most.

My advice to you is to find your gatekeepers. We all need help with all kinds of things in this life, and setting and maintaining your boundaries is no different.

Reflection: Invest in Meaningful Relationships

In a lot of ways, all this is adding up to investing in meaningful relationships—ones that foster joy. Some relationships can look like that on the surface, like my CRPS Facebook group, but they turn out to be the opposite. So how do we recognize the good ones?

Meaningful relationships start with emotional support through the good times and the bad. My friends can call me when they're excited about something or when they're stressed, sad, or disappointed, and I can do the same. No matter what, I can be emotionally there for them, and they can emotionally be there for me.

It's also important to spend time around the right people. Surround yourself with others who are seeking emotional growth. They're the ones who have their finger on the pulse of positivity—and the ones who will help you catch yourself when you're slipping into a negative mindset. Even better, they'll help you switch back into a positive one. That's what it's like in my Mastermind group. They're the family I've been looking for my whole life—what I hoped I might find, I think, in the CRPS Facebook group—and being around them increases my happiness and fulfillment.

Sometimes, the right relationships bring opportunities. They can also bring you health benefits. People who are worth investing in are often health-conscious individuals, or even health professionals, who inspire others to take steps in healthy directions.

Being able to share goals and values with the people around you is huge. I hosted my annual event while writing this book, and I was so inspired to see so many women in attendance boldly talking about their faith. It was emotional, and it was awesome, and it fostered love and authenticity among the people there. Let me tell you—the Holy Spirit was in that room. Sharing goals and values enables you to drop all your walls and be vulnerable. Me, I discovered this, at least in part, during my sobriety journey. Seeing others be vulnerable and allowing myself to be vulnerable in front of them helped me connect on a deeper level.

Above all else, building the right relationships in your life means listening to your gut and your heart. That's where you'll feel it, where you'll start to know whether a person is coming to you for the right reasons. Being in success means people will show up just to ride your coattails. I had an assistant who seemed amazing on paper, but it wasn't long before I realized she only wanted to work for me to get close to the successful and famous people I know.

There should be a flow of positive energy and support that goes both ways between you. If all the energy between you is flowing from you to the other person and never coming back, that relationship isn't right. In that same vein, look at a person's motives. Are they there to support you, or just to take from you?

Nurture relationships with people who would walk into a room and say nice things about you.

Look for people who make you feel good, emotionally and physically.

Look for the person who will hold the trash can for you when you need to throw up—that friend who you can let into your struggles because you know they won't use it against you.

Do you have that friend in your life? If you do, chances are that you know they're the friend who feels like home when you're around them. You can put on your robe, wash off your makeup, and just let down.

Who's the Sucker Here?

One last thing—consider it a good-natured reality check. When you personally invest in relationships, is your first thought what you can do for that person, or is it what they might be able to do for you? Are you the person who walks into the room to build somebody up, or are the first words out of your mouth gossip and negativity?

Think about it this way: if you can't spot the energy vampire in the room, there's a good chance it's *you*.

Actionable Steps

Identify your energy vampires. Who leaves you feeling exhausted and worn down? Who seems to cling to you just so they can complain? Who sees your positivity and your energy and sucks you dry, always wanting more, more, more? Identify these people in your life so you can take action to protect your well-being.

Set boundaries. Set boundaries where you need them and where they'll serve you best. This could be boundaries for your time, location, availability, or mental real estate.

It's also good to acknowledge that sometimes, even when we set the right boundaries in a relationship, we still have to get really strict and tough with someone who's stuck in their negativity. I always offer solutions first, but with an energy vampire that often won't ever be enough. "Hey, look," I'll say, "you realize you're complaining about the same thing over and over, but not doing anything about it, right? Either shit or get off the pot."

Embrace the power of no. In my line of work, I have people who will email or direct message me nonstop. *I want to be on your show, I want to be on your show, I want to be on your show.* I've learned to set boundaries with that wonderful word, *no*. First I give them a polite no, and then, when they keep on and keep on, I don't feel the pressure to answer. I simply delete, delete, delete. Bless and block. I've already answered them; I'm not going to give any of my energy or time to someone who doesn't respect the boundary I've set. And believe me, I LOVE having people on my show, but people whom I have built a relationship with or I have experienced their work.

Learn what fuels your joy fires. What gives you that spark? That fire in your belly? What promotes your feelings of peace and joy?

I think it begins with knowing our self-worth. We need to be mindful about who we are and what we need mentally, spiritually, and physically. When we do, it becomes easier to set boundaries to protect the good in our lives. Knowing who you are and what your values are can help you see when somebody in your life doesn't share those values. And then, when it's necessary, you can bless 'em and block 'em.

Invest in relationships that foster joy. Constant support, understanding, vulnerability, and energy that flows both ways are the cornerstones of relationships that foster joy. Get in the trenches with someone who'll get in the trenches with you.

Key Takeaway

Energy is everything and everything is energy. Learn how to distinguish the energy vampires in your life and set boundaries in those relationships.

9

Mind–Body Harmony

Cultivating Physical and Mental Well-Being for Lasting Joy

Mind–body harmony involves a state of flow between the mind and the body. It takes a deep awareness between the interconnectedness of your mental, emotional, and physical well-being. And that awareness begins with being mindful of the present moment. What are your thoughts, your emotions, your sensations, your physical experience? In other words, awareness involves really tuning into the body's signals and listening to its needs.

Why? Because your body will whisper to you, and then it will scream.

I should know, right? And let me tell you—I'm still learning this. Still experiencing it. It happened at the event I talked about in Chapter 8. Well, I needed my wonderful gatekeeper so badly because my body was whispering and I wasn't listening. *It's go time*, I thought. *I can't slow down*, I thought. *I can't stop and kick my leg up when I'm the emcee, and doing two keynotes, and introducing 20 people from the stage.*

My body saw things differently. It did not care that I was busy or under pressure or any of that. It kept whispering, and eventually the pain was so bad, I was forced to dash to the bathroom so I could throw up.

Puking from pain is never something I'm proud of, and I don't like people feeling sorry for me. But in that moment, sweaty and shaking over a toilet, I was so *angry*. I didn't even make it to lunch. I'd known the whole day that I needed to get off my leg—that I'd needed just a minute to acknowledge the pain and then maybe eat something—but let myself stay in the frame of mind that just said *go and go and go*.

As Bessel van der Kolk says in *The Body Keeps the Score*, our bodies will try and nudge us toward paying attention. But if we don't listen to those little signals it sends, our bodies will also stop us dead in our tracks.

Mind–body harmony is ever-changing. Imbalances can arise as a result of stress or disconnection, and when they do, we need to take steps to restore equilibrium. But if I'm being honest, I don't know that perfect balance is something anyone can achieve. I think the more accurate thing is to say it's always changing and flowing. Our job is to be in tune with our spiritual, physical, emotional, and mental needs and have practices in place to address things when they get out of whack.

Self-Care Isn't One-Size-Fits-All

When my mind–body harmony isn't flowing, it usually means I need to take better care of myself. When I get stuck in the loop of working like a dog nonstop, I miss those workouts.

I miss recovery meetings. I get fantastically irritable, and become a non-nice person. I know when I'm driving down the road and I start yelling at other drivers (when I'm in the car by myself, no less) that I need to stop and assess what's going on. Why am I so irritable? What do I need to change?

Truth be told, I probably need to fill my spiritual cup by going to a meeting or to church. I need to make sure I'm taking time to rest.

Maintaining a harmonious inner ebb and flow takes nurturing the right parts of yourself at the right times. Yes, self-care can be seasonal. There are seasons of hustle and recovery in my life as an entrepreneur. The thing about those seasons and mind–body harmony is that each one requires nurturing a different aspect of myself to keep the ebb and flow moving in the right direction.

And if one part of my self-care is missing, it affects every other thing. When I miss a workout, I miss out on movement that helps me stay positive, confident, and feeling good. When I miss the release of endorphins that comes from physical activity, it won't be long before I start to feel it emotionally. Inevitably, I will start getting depressed.

When my youngest daughter was born, for instance, I had to have a cesarian. Afterward, I couldn't run or work out for six weeks because my physical body needed to heal from the procedure. Alright, fine.

Meanwhile, my emotions were going wild—and not in a good way.

I'd been used to running five miles a day and working out. In fact, I was still running, hiking, and doing kettlebell workouts up until the night before Ruby was born. To go from all that to nothing was really difficult.

After a while, my husband suggested I talk to a therapist to help me feel better. Albeit a bit grudgingly, I went. "I know if I can just work out, I'll feel better," I told her.

She promptly told me I needed to be on antidepressants.

"If you think you need to work out to feel better, there's something wrong with you," she said.

Look—I'm not here to give therapy or antidepressants a bad name. Both are good and incredibly helpful when the fit is right. That said, sometimes you have to kiss a lot of frogs to find the therapist who's right for you and your needs. Me, I needed to find someone who would really listen to what I was saying and understand a bit more about my circumstances and personality before jumping straight to medication.

Well, long story short, I didn't take the antidepressants. I did start working out. And I felt better, just like I knew I would. My point is this: don't ignore the advice of your medical professionals, but do understand how interconnected your physical health is to your mental and emotional well-being. When you move your body, it helps in so many ways beyond physical strength. Moving your body also moves your mood.

So many people ask me how I can do all the things I do when I have complex regional pain syndrome (CRPS). "I have CRPS, I'm in a wheelchair, and I can't walk or work out," I hear. They all want to know what I take for the pain. I think in their own way, most people are looking for the magic pill. But listen, no single pill is going to change your whole life. Focusing on all you can do nutritionally, spiritually, mentally, and physically is the best way to move that needle.

And you know something? Only you know what it takes for you.

Only I know what I need to do in order to be my best self. I've done a lot of work to learn what those things are, and now I can say with certainty that it takes waking up earlier than anybody else in my family. It takes gifting myself with that time—before the daily onslaught of texts and emails begins—to read out of my daily journal, gather my thoughts, set my intentions, pray, and write my gratitude list. It takes working out every day and eating foods that fuel my body and my spirit and my mind.

I know if I don't do those things, I will wind up in a bathroom stall, puking my guts up when I should be lunching with attendees.

I encourage you to find those things for you. What nourishes and rejuvenates your body? Is it meditation, yoga, breathing exercises? I do box breathing exercises in the car when I'm sitting at stoplights. I take breaks from screen time to be in nature or just go find Ruby in the barn and give her horse a hug. All those self-care things bring me joy. Each time I do them, I come back a new person.

HALT and Cultivate Resilience

My whole life, I was always about the grit. I was always about the go go go. But we need more grace. Sometimes we move too fast and we don't get enough rest, but at the same time, we need to take more action and do less talking. We need to have less fear and more faith, less willpower and more good habits to rely on. People always assume I have this superstrong willpower. Well, no. I know better than anyone that you can't rely on willpower alone.

Why? Because willpower will get you nowhere if you're too hungry, angry, lonely, or tired. Those four things make me HALT. Be in any one of them for too long and your willpower goes out the window.

Case in point: yesterday, I hadn't eaten all day. I didn't get enough sleep. When I got home, there was a box of Crumbl cookies sitting on the kitchen counter. I walked past the box. Did I go the fridge and get the salad I knew was in there? Nope. But I sure did open that Crumbl box and eat a cookie instead.

Depending on willpower doesn't work. It takes good habits and discipline every single day.

For me, depending on willpower is a lot like wishful thinking. It's a lot like saying I'm going to manifest something in my life through my thoughts alone. Malarky. Wishing will get you nothing and nowhere. It's wonderful to have dreams, but you have to take steps toward making them happen by creating good habits out of our good intentions. I think Nike said it best.

Just do it.

Look—mind–body harmony is like a muscle we can strengthen, but we have to strengthen it before we need it. One of the biggest advantages of prioritizing self-care to maintain mind–body harmony is that you will have greater resilience in the face of challenges. You're going to be able to adapt to stressors. You aren't going to be yelling at people on the road. You'll be able to cope with adversity and maintain an inner peace during challenges.

I know that because doing the work is how I remain centered regardless of what's happening around me. The practices I follow on a daily basis to promote my mind–body harmony is what enables me keep my inner peace while I'm puking in the bathroom, and hosting 20 different speakers on my stage, and coordinating vendors and sponsors. In the midst of all of that, it's like, *Yeah, we got this. We are in control over here.*

Find What Works

Great, you might be thinking, *but I don't know what fuels my joy. I don't know how to figure it out. I don't know where to start.*

I can relate. When I started my business, I didn't have the money to invest in some big branding or marketing agent. I didn't have money to hire a publicist or anyone else to help me. I had to figure out for myself what was going to work for me online, so I started posting on Facebook and Instagram.

Before too long, I realized that Instagram was working for me. But I never would've known that if I hadn't just *started taking action.* I had to actually try something.

See, the same things that work for our business also work for our mind–body harmony: *you won't know what works for you until you try something.* I have a whole long list of things that I've tried for CRPS. Many, many of them didn't work, but I wouldn't have found the ones that did if I hadn't been willing to try things. That's also how I discovered that doing push-ups and prayer before I walk out on stage helps me get focused. Those two things in combination make me feel good and connect my mind, body, and spirit.

If you're trying to discover what works for you, it's important to set aside a time to explore. Maybe it's a nightly ritual, maybe it's a morning one. But I can pretty well guarantee it isn't doom-scrolling on your phone.

We've all done that, but it doesn't work. It doesn't build you up or energize you or help you post things your followers care about. All it does is drag your focus away from what you need to get yourself mentally, emotionally, and physically centered and put you in comparison mode. That's not inspiring you to be better. It's making you feel like you're less than what you see.

And look—you don't need that. You need to be the best person you can be for others. You need to be the best leader and the best example for your family. You need to be that person who shows up on social media with your own ideas because you're not distracted by all this other noise out there in the wilds of the internet.

And you *can* be all those things.

You just have to find what works for you.

Reflection: Protect Your Purpose and Keep Moving Forward

From time to time, people ask me if I would take anything back about my life. Would I change anything if I could? My answer is pretty straightforward.

"I don't get caught up in that."

Instead, I focus on what I can learn from my circumstances. If I let myself get caught up in asking myself why I was in that motorcycle accident or why I got diagnosed with CRPS, I would miss all the opportunities for healing and growth those two things have brought me.

I would also miss all the ways they've enabled me to help others, and that's where I'm truly fulfilled.

I believe we meet every single person for a reason. Everything happens for a reason. We might not know that reason yet, but it all comes together for our greater good—our purpose—if we just keep focusing on what we learned. Instead of asking "why me?" we should ask "what's next?"

Take that time I threw up at my event, for instance. I could've sat there and thought *Oh, why is this happening?* But if I'd done that, I would have started down the road to self-pity. That's the fastest way I know to derail a person from fulfilling their purpose.

So instead—and I'll credit all the daily work I do to keep my mind–body harmony ebbing and flowing in the right way for this one—my first thought was, *What can I do about the fact that I just threw up in the middle of my event? What's next? How can I move forward?*

I hate to say, "suck it up," but sometimes that's exactly what we have to do. And that is so much easier if we've been disciplined about keeping our mind–body harmony in check.

And we need that to protect our purpose.

Because the reality is this: pain will push you until your passion pulls you. My pain pushed me until I tapped into my passion, and now that passion is what pulls me forward.

Actionable Steps

Focus on your mental well-being. Shine a light on any shame you feel and let go of it. Learn the part you played in it and look at what you can change. Set healthy boundaries so you can take time for your own mental health. Get radically honest with yourself and take a good hard look at what isn't working.

Have people you can confide in, whether that's a sponsor, a mentor, a good friend who will call you out, or a therapist. I have them all!

Focus on your physical well-being. Make an appointment with your doctor and follow their advice. Bloodwork, taking supplements, drinking more water, and prioritizing sleep can all be intentional, effective parts of your business strategy. Set healthy boundaries so you can take time for your own physical health.

Focus on your spiritual well-being. Pray and attend church (even if it's online) and get in nature. Recommit to your gratitude or other practices if you've gotten off track. Attend a meeting, such as a 12 step recovery meeting, and establish accountability with your sponsor. Establish your areas of spiritual focus and regularly check in with your spiritual wellness.

Key Takeaway

Everything you do is either helping move you closer to your personal, health, and professional goals or it's hurting you.

CHAPTER

10

Thriving in Transition
Embracing Change as a Catalyst for Personal Growth

The whole world changed in 2020. Why is it that some people got depressed and stuck there while others seemed to still find joy?

I was still living in California and working with clients in person when the pandemic hit. You remember what happened: most public spaces shuttered. We were all supposed to stay home, and stay six feet away from everyone else if we had to go out. Lockdown was especially intense and long-lasting in California, where gyms were still closed after a year. Many went out of business.

I'm not sure anyone could have guessed that gyms—and everything else—would be closed for that long. But early on, another trainer I worked with decided to wait it out. She didn't want to start training her clients again until things got "back to normal."

She wasn't alone in that feeling. When the pandemic entered the picture, so many people wanted to hit "pause" and wait until things felt more familiar and comfortable before trying to move forward again. Often, these were the people who made excuses, who lived in fear of change. Instead of focusing on the solutions, they focused on excuses. But when you do that, negativity will sabotage everything.

"You can't wait," I told my friend. "You have to do something *now*."

I was as sure of that as I was of anything in my life, and it was what I planned to do. (When you come at me to complain, be warned: unless you come with a solution, you can't come with your negativity.) Within a week I'd shifted all my clients to Zoom, and to this day, I still even do personal fitness training with one of them.

When presented with an unfamiliar or uncomfortable situation, I think a lot of people are tempted to ask a dangerous question: *What if something goes wrong?*

That's the knee-jerk reaction, right? I get it. I've had practice with change, and I can tell you it is never easy. My transition from California to Texas was difficult (but enlightening). And I'm not a technology person, so my transition to virtual sessions wasn't a smooth one. A lot of things that could've gone wrong . . . and, well, they did. And I'm going to tell you about them in the coming pages.

But when you're tempted to ask what could go wrong, I challenge you to reroute your thoughts. Instead, think of what could happen if you asked different questions: *What if something goes right? What is the best thing that could happen if I lived my life in curiosity and excitement? What if I focused on new possibilities instead of focusing on what's broken?*

I'll tell you what.

When we do that, we can focus on what we can rebuild, on how we can grow, and on what sparks our joy.

Begin Where You Are

As I was changing gears and working with clients over Zoom, I was also building my speaking career. But suffice it to say, I was not one of those speakers who was freaking out and asking for donations on social media. Yes, some events at which I had been hired to speak were canceled. But instead of going, *Oh, I'm not going to be able to speak or travel*, I focused on solutions. What could I do?

For the people who are scared of transitions or change, that's where I suggest you begin. What can you do? What are your options? What things do you really enjoy doing?

Start where you are.

Use what you have.

Do what you can.

That's what I did in 2020, and my career *boomed*. I was still training clients, but I was also getting booked every week to speak. At my suggestion, many of the events moved from in-person to virtual ones.

Okay, I thought.

I didn't have the whole "speaking from home" thing all figured out. I knew it would be challenging, even difficult at times. But I needed to work through the pandemic—and all its tricky shifts to technology—so I could succeed.

Well, I didn't have certain things in my home studio. I didn't own a desktop computer—I only had a laptop. Alright, fine. I dragged a card table into my house, got a cardboard box to raise my laptop screen to eye level, and ordered a ring light. Boom. My setup was a far cry from state-of-the art, but I *was* set up.

Right away, I started doing virtual events.

The first one went horribly wrong. My camera stopped working; none of the attendees could see me. It was a disaster.

I could've let that be my last virtual event. I could've acknowledged the failure and stopped trying. Instead, I kept trying and failing. I remember trying to figure out how to create slides (it was like reading Greek); I remember getting on a virtual event thinking I would see all the attendees, but only seeing my own face (it was far more discombobulating than I would've thought); I remember trying to figure out how to interact with attendees in comments to fix an issue (namely, that they could only see my face when I wanted them to see my slides). All of that was just one event.

In other words, the learning curve wasn't always pretty, but I did learn from my mistakes.

And do you know what happened? People kept calling me, and I kept booking events. I improved with each one, and eventually the event planner from my first virtual speaking gig became a client of mine. She hired me again, and I spoke at another event for her while I was working on this book.

Don't Be Perfect, Be Human

One day early in my career, I asked Johnny and Ruby to leave the house while I gave a talk. At the time, I had the wrong kind of microphone and it picked up every little noise—the dishwasher, a lawnmower outside. You name it, you could hear it. But this was a big event, and I wanted things to be extra quiet. Professional. So I planned for everything that day . . . except for my little dog, Goldie.

Who started barking like crazy to go outside as soon as I started my presentation.

For a fleeting moment, I wondered if I could pretend Goldie wasn't barking her head off and just keep going. I could finish my talk and *then* let her out, right?

But I knew I wasn't fooling anyone. There was nothing for it but to name the tiny barking elephant in the virtual room.

"Y'all can hear that, can't you?" I asked.

Everyone burst out laughing, saying things like, "Oh! Amberly's human, too!"

Truthfully, it was a relief to let that particular guard down. I don't *want* people to think I have it all figured out. I am definitely not perfect. I mess up all the time. And really, sometimes things are just *messy*. Imperfect. But you just keep going. You move forward. And the beautiful thing is, you can learn from your mistakes.

Eventually I learned to keep the door cracked for Goldie. Eventually I got a better computer and lighting and made sure my background was set up in a way that looked professional. I always say, thank goodness we don't have to have it all figured out. Perfection isn't a requirement. It's up to you to decide to own your power by thinking about what you can do in any given situation.

Hitting my stride on social media was another huge learning curve. I didn't know what I was doing when I started posting. All I knew was that I had a vision to help others and a message to share. So I decided that I would do whatever I could to get that message out there and committed to posting five days a week no matter what. I was going to share my message, and that was that. I kept at it.

I still didn't know what I was doing.

For starters, I still didn't know how to write a caption. My pictures were equally terrible. Suffice it to say I was not one of those people who joined Instagram and immediately got thousands of likes on anything and everything I posted.

In fact, in those early days I remember getting excited when I got double-digit likes.

Go digging at the bottom of my Instagram today and you'll still see all those crappy first posts. I leave them up so people can see that we all start from somewhere. We make mistakes, but that's how we learn and grow.

That's uncomfortable for a lot of people. The thought of making mistakes can even be paralyzing for some. *Oh, I can't mess up*, they think. *Everything has to look perfect. I can't get turned down*. But listen—making a mistake or having a failure or two is not something to be afraid of. It can even be something to look forward to because it will help you figure out what not to do next time.

If there's one thing I can say about learning from a mistake, it's that the experience leaves you with a lesson you'll never forget. I can truly say the things I've failed at have been my greatest lessons. I want you to be able to learn from my mistakes, too. Then you won't have to make 'em. But if you do, remember that every mistake and failure will help you get farther down the road and closer to where you want to be.

My years as a professional dancer helped me change my perspective on making mistakes and hearing no. Looking back, it's easy to see how auditioning—and being constantly rejected— helped me become a better entrepreneur because I stopped looking at no as a deterrent. *Okay, good*, I think when I hear it. *I'm one step closer to a yes.*

Don't make the mistake of translating a no as "I just wasn't good at that" or "I guess that thing I wanted to do or be isn't meant for me." We all get to hear no, we all get butterflies and nervousness. I get that. Following our passions and chasing down our dreams is scary business.

But if we let those things stop us, we'll never go anywhere.

Embracing change can do so much for us, and it begins with embracing a growth mindset. A growth mindset views challenges as opportunities for learning rather than as obstacles. A growth mindset asks, "What can I learn from this?"

That question opens the door to empowerment because it enables you to approach obstacles with curiosity and resilience instead of fear and uncertainty.

Embracing change ignites a sense of excitement and curiosity, sparking joy along our continual journey of evolution and empowerment. When you embrace the ebb and flow of life's transitions, you will find yourself not merely surviving them but thriving in the ever-changing currents of experience.

By rejecting change as an obstacle and viewing it as an opportunity for growth, you unlock your potential for personal development and self-discovery. As we navigate through uncertainty with resilience and adaptability, each transition becomes a stepping stone toward a more fulfilling and authentic existence.

Focus on the bad and we feel down, get anxious, turn to unhealthy habits, and worse. Focus on the good, and the good just gets better.

When we focus on what we can do instead of what we can't do, it's alchemy.

Reflection: Embracing Change to Spark Joy

So, how does embracing change spark joy? When I think about that, my mind immediately jumps back to experiencing the pandemic in Southern California, when everything was shut down and we were all homebound for so long. The gyms weren't open. Nothing was open.

And you know by now how much I love working out—and how much I need to be able to do it.

Well, going to the gym was out. I could've sat at home feeling sorry for myself that the gym was closed, but that wasn't going to solve anything. And anyway, Amberly = action. So I embraced the changes around me and approached the challenge with curiosity. How could I get a gym-worthy workout without leaving my house?

That's how my husband came home and found me in the backyard.

Leg pressing our outdoor furniture.

"What are you doing?" he asked, shocked.

"I can't go to the gym," I ground out between presses, "but I can pick up this old sofa."

Turns out, leg-pressing the big ottoman we had outside was a great way to escape the pandemic, even for a little while. So was doing hamstring curls and planks with my daughter's skateboard, and unearthing my old tap shoes. I hadn't had them on since before my accident, and I wasn't sure if I could still tap at all.

"Oh, Mom," Ruby said when she saw what I was doing, "I don't think those shoes are going to fit you anymore."

Well, I thought, *let me see if I can try*.

Lucky for me, they did fit. And in a flurry of doing anything and everything I could, I got out my phone to film myself dancing for the first time since the accident.

"I'm not on TikTok," I said to Ruby by way of explanation.

"Mom, you do not want to be on TikTok. You're too old for TikTok."

"Oh? Well now I'm *definitely* going to do it."

I turned my camera on, did a dance, and set the scene for anyone who watched my video. "This is the first time I've done a tap dance since my motorcycle accident," I said.

Well, that video went viral. People went crazy for it, and I had so many tell me I had inspired them to do the same—to just try something. For my part, I had fun.

So before long, I was picking up goats.

Yes, you read that right. When we lived in Los Angeles, we boarded our horse in Calabasas. Horseback riding was a wonderful way to maneuver the lockdowns because we were always at least six feet away from others while riding outdoors. And as a bonus, we could also keep goats at the same facility.

Turns out, the setup was great for working out. We kept our goats in a large field, and I would go out there, pick up a goat, and start doing squats. Bubba the goat was the biggest one in the herd, and he was my favorite one to exercise with. He liked it, too, I think, because he would see me coming and know it was squat time. He'd come straight to me.

Let me tell you—squatting with farm animals is a *ball*. We laughed and laughed and laughed, and it brought us so much happiness and joy during those unending months of lockdown.

I could've sat down and felt sorry for myself that the gym was closed. I could've rejected change like so many others.

But if I had, think of all that laughter and joy I would've missed out on.

Actionable Steps

Cast your vision for the future, then faithfully take small steps toward it every day. As you move through periods of change and transition, it's important to set clear, attainable goals. When I first started speaking virtually, a "Tony Robbins studio" wasn't attainable for me. But the cardboard boxes and laptop setup *was* attainable, so I set that goal for my studio and made it work.

Be obedient to the vision and plan for getting there. And don't forget to celebrate your victories along the way.

Surround yourself with a like-minded community. That's why I started my Mastermind group—so that people could have a community of like-minded people to confide in and learn from.

As my friend Greg Reid always says, "Seek counsel, not opinion." The difference is that everyone in your life is going to have an opinion about what you're doing—especially people who aren't doing the same things as you. These opinions generally aren't all that helpful, and sometimes they can be downright hurtful. But when we seek counsel, we're going to somebody who has already done the thing that we want to do and has been successful at it. That person is going to give you good, solid advice instead of their opinions about why what you want to do is impossible and can't be done.

Take action. Like my grandfather always said, "You have a shovel in your hand, you can pray for a hole, or you can start digging." You can't just pray that things will get better or that change will come. You have the power to improve your circumstances and create change. You just have to start digging.

Be patient and relentlessly consistent while you're in pursuit of breakthrough. Patience is something I constantly have to work on. I generally want to be able to have something done the first time or way I attempt it.

But patience is necessary because waiting for a breakthrough to happen is hard.

Really, really hard.

Breakthroughs could be anything. Me, I'm always wondering when I'm going to start feeling better. When the pain is going to ease up. When will I take the medication and experience antibiotics doing for me what they're meant to and getting an infection under control?

But there are other breakthroughs. *When will I be asked to speak onstage? When am I going to be part of the cool kids' club and be part of their upcoming events?* For a friend of mine who's been trying to get her book published for a long, long time, when will a publisher finally say yes; they want to give her a book deal? For another friend of mine, when will Mr. Right come along and help her step into the relationship she's always wanted?

Encourage yourself as you work to extend and develop patience while also—and this is key—being relentlessly consistent (because relentless consistency is exactly what it takes). Remind yourself that the breakthrough comes right after the test, and keep moving forward.

Learn to use your nerves. Put some harnesses on those butterflies in your stomach and let them lift you up. That's what I'm doing when I do push-ups and prayer before I go onstage to speak. And I always have the first 30 seconds of my talk memorized, too—that's my plan to get through the first moments of being onstage. Those 30 seconds lead me into the exercise of speaking, and it's smooth sailing from there.

Key Takeaway

Resilience doesn't mean bouncing back (even though that's how the dictionary defines it). Resilience is having the courage to move forward and live a life of happiness and joy even when things don't go as planned. Resilience is bouncing *forward*.

11

Gratitude Is Alchemy/ Gratitude in Action

How Practicing Gratitude Transforms Your Outlook on Life

When Ruby was younger, I always ended our day the same way. I'd hop in bed with her and ask, "What's the best thing that happened to you today? What's one thing you're grateful for?"

A lot of times, her answers were full of the glorious silliness of childhood. "I'm grateful that I was twerking today," she'd giggle.

"Ruby!"

I always pretended to be shocked, if not just so she'd let loose a new wave of giggles. It was always simple fun.

All silliness aside, I knew it was good for both of us. So much of how we end our day affects how we start our tomorrow.

When Life Gives You Lemons

As I continue down the path of life, what I do to feel and express my gratitude continues to evolve. Now, I have a dedicated gratitude practice, made up of three things: starting my day with gratitude, sharing that gratitude with my God Squad throughout the day, and messaging someone I'm grateful for. See, something magical happens when you get in the practice of remembering to think about all the things you're thankful for.

But don't we all have days when we wake up and things feel hard? I know I do. Some days I just feel bad, down, and can't stop beating myself up because I don't think I'm doing enough.

Thankfully, I have a group of ladies in Los Angeles—my six closest sober sisters—who I can rely on. They're my God Squad, and we use an app to write down 10 things we're grateful for each day. Then we share our gratitude lists with each other.

It's one thing to feel grateful and recognize feelings of gratitude and thankfulness. It's another thing to write them all down—in a journal, an app, wherever. The method doesn't matter as much as the act of committing your thoughts in writing.

Putting pen to paper (or fingertips to keyboard) is powerful. Not only do you remember your gratitude but you also actually *feel* it as you write it down. I recommend keeping those thoughts in a journal, or a jar, or a group chat, so you can go back to them when you're feeling low—and share them with others.

I've heard it said before that sharing is caring. Well, in the case of my God Squad, sharing is also *accountability*—something we all need to keep going when the going gets tough.

The days I wake up feeling like life is too hard are the days I'm most grateful for the accountability my God Squad provides. Knowing they've committed to this practice alongside me helps me change my perspective when things get rough. I might wake up feeling like there's nothing to be grateful for that day, but then

I think, *I have all the ladies in my God Squad.* That thought helps me get back to my gratitude baselines: *I'm alive. I can walk. I can share my story with others.* And, thanks to my God Squad, I can also read what others are grateful for.

It changes everything.

I remember one day in particular. I was having a bit of a pity party. *Life is so hard,* I thought. *I'm sick of being in pain.*

Well, a few minutes later, one of my sober sisters posted in our group chat. "Today is my last treatment," she wrote.

She just beat cancer, I thought, humbled. *I have a lot going on right now, but I don't have cancer. There's so much to be grateful for.* My sober sister's gratitude helped put everything in perspective.

The Lemonade Will Follow

Look—there are days when making my gratitude list feels like a chore. There are days when it feels like life is too hard and writing down all the things I'm thankful for is just one more thing on my to-do list. And I need that list to be shorter, not longer. I don't need that extra chore.

But you know what? The moment I start writing, I start feeling better.

A gratitude practice can be a lot like exercising when you'd rather be a couch potato or cooking healthy meals for yourself when you'd rather go through the drive-through. How many times have I thought, *Oh, I don't feel like working out.* Sometimes I'll even drive to the gym . . . and then sit in the parking lot . . . while I scroll through Instagram and think I could just . . . skip the gym that day.

But then I think of how I'm going to feel afterwards. If I work out, I'm going to feel better mentally. I'm going to get stronger and boost my confidence.

Well, my gratitude practice is like that, too.

I think it's the same with any kind of practice. It's all mind, body, spirit—interconnected, interdependent, and harmonized. I need practices that hit on all three of those things. If I don't, the harmony gets out of whack. So I can work out every day, but I also need to pray. (There's power in prayer, and I need to pray to help me focus on how I can feel better.)

The gratitude list helps me mentally, working out helps me physically, and prayer helps me spiritually. Keeping them in balance can be difficult, just like meal prepping and prioritizing other aspects of a healthy life. But there's an old saying: do the hard things first, and life gets easier. But when you take the easy way out, life just gets hard.

Reflection: Gratitude and Resilience

All those things that add up to good in your life—working out, eating healthy, and yes, your gratitude practice—will raise your emotional baseline to a higher level when you do them faithfully and consistently.

Your gratitude practice is just such a huge part of that. It will foster a positive outlook and turn what you *can't* do into what you *can*. It'll turn what's lacking in your life to what you have. And it will reduce feelings of envy or comparison because it gets you focused on all those things you actually have. In turn, that means it *also* helps reduce stress, anxiety, and depression. In general, gratitude promotes resilience, emotional well-being, and better health.

Actionable Steps

Keep a gratitude journal. Any kind or form of journal will do— even sticky notes that get tossed into a jar for safekeeping.

But if you'd like a guided journal experience, visit my website (www.amberlylago.com) and download my gratitude journal for free.

Don't self-edit your gratitude. My friend beating cancer was a wonderful thing, but overcoming or accomplishing something huge is not the threshold for gratefulness. There's no hierarchy of what "belongs" on your gratitude list. There are days when my list includes a hot cup of coffee, or that the sky is blue, or that it's raining and I get to hear the pitter-patter of raindrops on the roof. Sometimes it's that I get to drive my daughter to school and have that time with her. And, yes—other times, it's that I booked a speaking gig, or that I just got paid for one. No matter what it is, stopping and pausing to look around for things to add to the list really gets me in the present moment.

Start your practice with accountability. Find a friend, partner, sibling, or support group member who will commit to doing a gratitude practice with you.

When you're thankful for someone, tell them. I reach out to at least one person a day to tell them how grateful I am that they're in my life. Sometimes it's a friend, sometimes a family member, sometimes an individual who has played a role in my career. The thing is, you never know how telling someone you're thankful for them can affect their life. They could be going through a hard time, but hearing that someone is grateful for them can turn everything around.

Sometimes sharing gratitude isn't about how I feel, but how my gratitude could help someone else.

Just do it. This isn't rocket science. It's not that hard. That's by design—one of my mottoes is "just keep it simple." You don't have to overcomplicate things or get in your head (I know the temptation, believe me). I'm always thinking, *How can*

I do this differently? or *What's the best way to do this?* But it really is simple.

And you have the knowledge now—you just have to act on it.

Key Takeaway

A gratitude practice can change the way you think about your circumstances. It will train your thoughts and foster a positive outlook on life.

12

Radiating Joy to the World

Creating a Ripple Effect of Positivity and Happiness

Right before I began writing this chapter, I gave a talk to a group of businesswomen. *Oh my gosh*, I thought as I left the stage, *that was so horrible. That was the worst talk I have ever given.*

I thought I sucked. I thought I'd been too vulnerable in a room full of professionals. I was in my head so much that I actually woke up freaking out at 4:30 the next morning, my thoughts a constant loop of *That was so bad, so bad, so bad.* Fueling my internal spiral, I hadn't heard back from the planner afterwards. That fact seemed to confirm every negative feeling and assessment I had.

Well, the next morning, a gorgeous floral arrangement was delivered to my house. "Thank you for the presentation," the card read. It was from that event planner.

Here I've been all in my head—negative, hard on myself, and living in my worst-case scenario, I thought. Ruby was with me, and I showed her the flowers. "I guess it wasn't as bad as I thought," I said.

Wouldn't it be nice if a reassuring bouquet showed up to jolt us out of our negativity every time we started to spiral?

Challenging Negative Thoughts

When I'm encouraging someone out of their rut of negative thoughts so they can begin thinking positive ones, I always begin with practicing gratitude. As I've said before, practicing gratitude is alchemy, and it will totally transform the way you feel and how you see the world (not to mention how you see your life in the world). That said (again), there are other things you need to do if you want to radiate joy to the world.

Practicing positivity is also about challenging our negative thoughts and identifying where they're coming from. Why are you thinking that upsetting or mean thing about yourself? I also think that when we challenge our negative thoughts, it helps us identify our negative beliefs. Where did they come from? When did they start? Knowing those two things helps you disrupt those thoughts and switch them to positive ones.

They aren't always easy to identify when we're stuck in the loop, though. When we're in our heads, it's much easier to just tell ourselves the worst things. So often, it's necessary to talk the negativity out with someone and get some outside perspective on things. Surround yourself with uplifting people. That makes all the difference.

It also helps to set realistic goals and celebrate small victories along the way. It's easy to focus on big goals, but the small ones are just as important. We might hit 2 or 3 or 47 big goals in our lifetime, but forward progress in our daily lives is really made up of string after string of small goals.

Engage in activities that bring you joy. That's something I forget to do sometimes. As much as I love going to the gym—and as much as I know I need to work out to stay positive and joyful—sometimes I get busy and Johnny has to remind me to go. "What's going on," he'll ask. "You haven't been going to the gym." (See, that's a one-two punch of surrounding yourself with uplifting people—so they can remind you to do the things that bring you joy.)

There are also times when we all need to seek professional help through counseling and therapy. I might not have found the therapist who was right for me when I had postpartum depression after Ruby was born, but I eventually did. Sometimes you have to kiss a lot of frogs. Eventually, I found a therapist who was more attentive and listened. They were better for me and more attuned to my needs.

I'm a big believer that what we think and what we believe is what we attract in our life. Those things become what we achieve. The more we focus on the things we want, the closer we get to attaining them.

Remember, thinking positively isn't about ignoring bad things and pretending they're not happening. It's acknowledging them, then accepting them, then taking actionable steps to change them.

Positive Thoughts and Self-Love

What is the connection between thinking positive thoughts and practicing self-love and forgiveness? I think that when you have positive thoughts—when you are, as I like to say, practicing positivity—you are actually practicing a form of self-love.

I grew up around a few glass-half-empty, pessimistic people. They were important, influential figures in my life, and they left me with a crystal-clear understanding: *I don't ever want to be that way.*

A lot of people think I'm naturally positive all the time, but the truth is, I'm not. I have to work at it. But because I have worked at it, I'm equipped to handle negative experiences. For instance, I had a client who sometimes referred to me as *Pollyanna*, the sunshine-only child heroine from the Disney movie of the same name. (When someone calls you a Pollyanna, it's not typically a compliment—and it wasn't when it came from this client, who always wanted to complain.) But when she said something negative, I had the ability to think around that thought and look at the positive in the situation.

I think we can train our brains to do that—to look at the positive. But I know that when I'm in a negative place, I just beat myself up even more. In those moments, like the one I described experiencing after my talk, I don't feel like I'm deserving of self-love or taking care of myself.

In fact, that feeling happens to me a lot. I gave another talk while working on this chapter, and as part of the event, I was supposed to attend a VIP dinner the Friday evening before. The only problem was, I was in so much pain Friday that I could barely walk. I had no business going anywhere but to rest, but the pain was clouding my judgment and all I could think about was getting to that dinner. *I won't drive*, I thought. *I'll get an Uber*.

A few minutes later when my Uber arrived, I walked outside to meet it. Johnny came out to see me off, but when he looked at me his expression changed.

"Amberly," he said, "you are in no place to go to this dinner. You've worked so hard to build your brand, but right now you don't look like yourself. Your eyes are glossed over. You're not thinking right."

Thankfully, I have a husband willing to stop me and tell me I need to rest. If he hadn't, I probably would've gone to that event and experienced an in-person version of the Instagram Live debacle that caused me so much heartache and shame. He was right. I needed to stay home.

I reluctantly called the event planner. "I'm so sorry," I said. "I can't come to the VIP dinner. I'll rest up tonight and show up big for you tomorrow."

Well, the next day I was still in a lot of pain. It wasn't as bad as it had been the day before, but it was bad enough that adrenaline wasn't even enough to kick it like usual. My body was shaking. I wound up asking to use a headset microphone instead of a handheld mic because I was afraid people would see my hands shaking so much.

As you can probably imagine, I did not feel like I was on my game. I didn't feel like I did a great job. I did my best considering the circumstances, but afterwards—and for the rest of the day—I just sat and beat myself up.

I compared myself to every other speaker. And when I got home, instead of celebrating that I'd just had this event—and gotten to speak at all—all I did was think, *You suck. See, you're not meant for this career after all.* I didn't feel like I deserved to take a bubble bath or give myself a break. I almost felt like I needed to punish myself for not doing well.

I think that when you have positive self-talk, your ability to plan for your day goes through the roof. You can take control of your schedule; plan to take time for the things your mind, body, and spirit need; and prioritize your health.

That was my only path out of the negativity I was stewing in after that event.

I started and ended my day on a good note with positive self-talk and prayer. I read from my daily reflections book early in the morning, and then I went to the gym. I made sure I took my supplements and did everything I could mentally, spiritually, and physically. And finally, my inner critic calmed down. That night, I slept for the first time. I woke up feeling better and ready for the day.

Overall, thinking positively can really serve as a foundation for us for practicing self-love and forgiveness. And it really involves treating ourselves with kindness, understanding, and compassion. When we do that, we can better serve other people. And we are also an example for others to do the same.

Cultivate a Positive "Soulset"

I think so much of the foundation we build for ourselves begins with how we feel in our soul—what I think of as our "soulset." Next comes our mindset, which affects how we show up and how we treat ourselves. It all goes hand in hand. Like I've said time and again, no single thing will make or break you. One thing affects another thing, which affects another thing, which affects another thing.

A good friend of mine has recently had a lot of extreme pain. He has finally gotten rid of it, but he struggled with it for a long time. "I've always been a driven person," he told me. "I've always been highly focused. But now, with no pain, I feel superhuman. I'm twice as productive."

I wanted to cry because I really relate to that. *Imagine what I could do if I didn't have pain*, I thought. *If I can do all this* with *pain, can you imagine how I could show up in the world if I didn't have it? What kind of impact I could make?* But we do our best with what we have.

We nurture our soulset.

Soulset for me comes from being still, from just taking a pause and having a moment to really listen to your soul—what you need, what your desires are, and what your body needs from you.

My whole life, I was in fight mode. I was determined to fight the pain, whether it was emotional or caused by complex regional pain syndrome (CRPS). And it took me a long time to just let go, be in surrender, and make sure my soul was okay. But gradually, I could take those moments to just be still and listen and anchor myself to God.

Once I could do that, I could also ask God to walk with me throughout the day. I could release my self-will—that urge I always had to accomplish anything and everything on my own. Part of that will gave me grit, and I relied on grit for many, many years. But the thing is, when I only rely on grit, it doesn't mean I'm stronger or more capable. It just means I've kind of exhausted all other avenues to the point that I feel like I only have myself to rely on.

But self-will can only get me (or you) so far because true happiness comes from connection—to others, to your soul, to your values, to God. That's why my idea of success is being able to do the things you love with the people you love—it's what sparks joy.

Positive Thoughts, Stronger Agency

Thinking positively helps us embrace our agency in our own life and results in transformation and hope. It encourages people to focus on the things they're grateful for—even the small things. Like I said before, the more we focus on the good, the more the good comes in our life. It's kind of like being pregnant—all you see is pregnant women. Or like buying a new car—all you see on the road is the same make and model that's now in your driveway.

Tony Robbins does an amazing exercise when he's speaking that involves his entire audience. He asks everyone to look around the room and find as many things as they can that are the color red. After a minute, he asks everyone to close their eyes. "Okay," he says, "now tell me what in the room was *blue*." Of course no one in the room can recall anything around them that was blue. They've been too focused on what's red.

For me, that's how positive thinking works. When you're focused solidly on what's positive, you see the positive things. You get more positive opportunities because that's the energy you're putting out into the universe. People feel that energy and are drawn to it.

Practicing positive thoughts also increases our resilience and enhances our motivation. It improves our relationships and boosts our confidence. Thinking positive will help you flip the script when you're feeling low and take action that will empower you to feel confident. It helps you believe in your ability and your potential because it really enables you to problem-solve and see challenges as opportunities for growth and learning, leading you to more creative and effective problem-solving strategies. Positivity enables you to take a step back and ask, *What can I do? What do I need?* and take back the power you have in your own life.

Thinking positive especially creates resilience in adversity. In challenging times or catastrophic ones, a community you've built with a culture of positivity will band together around you and offer support and resilience in the face of those challenges so that you can emerge stronger than before.

Being positive doesn't mean you won't have hard times or challenges. It just means that when you have them, you can get through them faster and stronger.

Reflection: Create Ripples of Positivity

When I finally learned how to accept all my scars, I remember doing a post for the first time on Instagram. I had no makeup on,

I was wearing my glasses and shorts and a sweatshirt, and I just took a quick selfie with my scars showing.

Well, that post went viral.

Let me tell you—more people comment and approach me after my talks about that post than any other. They thank me for my vulnerability and authenticity, for just showing up without trying to pretend everything is perfect. That's what the world needs from me and you—positivity without pretending perfection. People in the world gravitate toward that because they want a solution.

When we accept ourselves, flaws and all, we are fostering that solution. We become walking permission slips for other people to do the same. When we own our imperfections, dance with abandon and silliness, laugh out loud and cry our tears, we give others permission to do the same.

And the permission we give goes even farther. Someone could see me working out and think, *Well, if Amberly can do this with CRPS, maybe I can, too. If Amberly can really wear shorts and show her scars, maybe this scar on my knee isn't so bad. Maybe I can love my mastectomy scars and feel confident and sexy again.*

A woman reached out to me over Instagram to tell me that she'd had had a double mastectomy. She opened up to me about having surgery, and then getting implants, and how the implants had been causing issues for her. Because I had shown my scars in positivity and acceptance, she said, she completely transformed her life. She had her implants removed and was in total acceptance. As a result of being in that acceptance, her business grew (she is an expert yogi with a huge following) and she began doing retreats. I didn't grow her business, and I'm not taking credit for all the things she's done. But it amazes me that a selfie I took had a ripple effect far beyond anything I could ever personally do.

Sometimes, the ripples stay a bit closer to home—but that doesn't make them any less profound.

A few years ago, Ruby and I were riding little razor scooters down the street. We were almost through a crosswalk when a car came flying through the intersection and hit both of us.

There is nothing scarier than seeing a car and knowing it's going to hit your child. I remember that I was a little bit ahead of Ruby; I flung out my hand between her and the car. Just so you know, putting out your hand does not stop a car from hitting your daughter.

I got thrown to the side and Ruby got thrown back. Thank God the car didn't roll over us. Still, it was the scariest thing ever.

We were taken to the hospital, of course, and we were seated near a woman in the emergency room who was just . . . not very positive or nice.

Ruby and I did things a little differently. Every time the doctors and nurses came over to Ruby and me, we said, "Thank you so much. I know this could have been so much worse, and I know you have your hands full with COVID. I just appreciate so much that you're taking good care of us."

I told anyone who would listen that I knew we were lucky. There we were, being treated for injuries we got by being hit by a car, and all I could talk about was how blessed we were.

I could see the ripple effect it had on the doctors and nurses. They kept bringing us crackers and apple juice (sadly, they didn't do that for the negative lady). "We're going to get you out of here as soon as we can," they said. "We just need to do a CAT scan to make sure your daughter's brain is okay."

Five hours later, they'd done the scan, given Ruby the all-clear, and we were on our way home. In ER time, that's basically magic.

For her part, Ruby—who could have been crying and freaking out—spent the day cutting up with me. We made jokes; we laughed and laughed. It's not that we weren't in pain—we were pretty scraped up, and I couldn't move that hand I'd thrown out in my attempt to protect Ruby because the car's impact burst a joint. But as we walked out of the hospital, Ruby said, "Mama, we got rolled in here on a gurney and we are walking out like champions."

I immediately thought of all those years I spent going in her bedroom at night to ask her about the best thing that happened to her that day and the one thing she was grateful for. Everything I'd done every day leading up to that accident helped her become the victor of her life instead of the victim.

How's that for a ripple effect of positivity? In our worst moments of pain and fear, we can still find joy.

And the thing is, you can see it happening. You can see the positive energy rippling out *every day*. The day before I sat down to write these words, I went to the deli counter at my local grocery store. Let me tell you—the guy who works that counter is usually pretty down and negative, so I always make it a point to roll up with a big smile on my face. "Hey man, how are you doing?" I'll ask. "What's going on?"

This particular day, he told me he was almost off work and he was ready to clock out. "I can't wait," he said.

"Well, that's good. What are you going to do?"

I didn't do or say anything out of the ordinary—I just talked to him in a positive way. Before I knew it, he handed me a bag of chicken for half off. I didn't do it for the extra chicken but I thanked him all the same.

Actionable Steps

Understand how your thoughts become your destiny.
Above all else, remember that your thoughts are powerful. They become your words. Your positive words become your

behavior. Keep your behavior positive because your behavior becomes your habits. Your habits become your values and your values become your destiny.

Keep your thoughts—then your words, then your behaviors, then your habits, then your values, and finally, your destiny—positive. Take charge of your thoughts by identifying what allows you to be positive. Me, if I haven't properly nourished myself with good food, or if I've strayed from my HALT (which stands for hungry, angry, lonely, tired) principles, the negative thoughts come in. I don't feel as good physically, emotionally, or mentally. I won't be able to think straight and I will begin to spiral.

In fact, depression runs in my family, but HALT has helped me to break that cycle. I just have to stick to it. For me, that looks like moving my body to move my mood, seeing a couple of friends at the gym and being able to smile and quickly connect with them, or even getting outside and getting my hands dirty in the garden and digging around, because feeling the dirt on my hands is incredibly therapeutic for me.

Recognize the agency you have in your own life. No, you can't control everything. Yes, sometimes you have to embrace the suck and keep your chin up. But that doesn't mean you're at the mercy of everything and everyone who isn't you. Life gets better when you decide it does.

Whatever it takes, train your thoughts on good things and watch your agency grow.

Loosen your grip on self-will. There's a third-step prayer I find so much help in releasing self-will. It says, "I offer myself to Thee to build with me and to do with me as Thou will. Relieve me of the bondage of self that I may better do Thy will. Take away my difficulties, that victory over them may bear witness to those I would help of Thy love, Thy power, Thy way of life. May I do Thy will in all."

Trade a hunk of that grit for connection—to your soul, to others, to God. You'll be glad you did.

Key Takeaway

Self-love is a process that takes time, but transformation is possible. Hope is available.

13

Bouncing Forward from Life's Hard Knocks

B ack in the days of Clubhouse, the social connections platform that blew up in popularity during the pandemic, I had my own club I created called the True Grit and Grace Club. Once a week I had a room for entrepreneurs and another room that was a support group for people who had chronic illnesses and complex regional pain syndrome (CRPS). I poured into those groups, and the members tried their hardest to stay positive, but I always left feeling completely drained. I began to notice that I dreaded going in those rooms to talk about pain. I knew the experience would intensify any pain I might have and drain me, mentally and emotionally.

Meanwhile, after being in the room of entrepreneurs I just felt different. When I left that room, I would be lit up with joy. I would be energized.

I looked forward to that room.

I think so much of what we focus on makes such a huge difference. People who are resilient focus on tools and tactics and solutions. People who lean into the victim mentality focus on all the things they can't do—what's wrong with their lives and what will never go right.

For some, I guess that works. Me, I ended up leaving the rooms that drained me because I want to build up my life with positivity and joy.

Having had that experience, I knew going in that this chapter would be the hardest for me to write.

In my first book, I talked about pain A LOT. Pain from my motorcycle accident, pain from my surgeries, pain from my recovery. There was physical pain, emotional pain, relationship pain—to the point that when it came time to write about my experience with CRPS, I thought, *I just can't bring myself to write about any more pain.*

When the book came out, some people were angry or disappointed by that choice. These were the people who bought my book thinking I was going to tell them all the things I did to get out of pain. But the thing is, *I'm still in pain.* I'm not a doctor, and as much as I can share the things that help with the pain, it might not work the same for you. I know some people who have had their lives changed by getting a spinal cord stimulator. For me, my body completely rejected that treatment. I don't even talk about CRPS as much on social media anymore, mainly because I realized that the more I talk about it, the more I feel the pain of it. The mind is so powerful, you know? As soon as I start talking about it and explaining how it feels, the pain intensifies in my foot. I feel it start to burn all the way up my leg.

But, deep breath.

Here we go.

Layers and Layers of the Worst of It

The pain I have from CRPS is the worst I've ever experienced in my life. It is harder than any accident or surgery has ever been. In fact, I would actually go back and endure another 34 surgeries if it meant I could one day live without CRPS.

As you know by now, this isn't my first rodeo when it comes to pain. From sexual, physical, and psychological abuse to all the accidents and surgeries I've endured, you could say I've . . . seen some stuff. (And that's just the short list. I've also been mugged. I have been hit by a car not once, not twice, but *three times*—once by the SUV that caused my motorcycle accident, once while riding scooters with Ruby, and another time when I was riding my bicycle. That time, I landed on the hood of the car that hit me.) CRPS is worse than all of it. I know, you might be thinking my next book should be called *Look Both Ways*.

From a purely physical perspective, nerve pain is the worst type of pain. Plain and simple, nerve pain just feels more severe and is harder to treat. It's hard to touch it with medications or therapies—I know because I've tried everything. Not only did I try all the treatments the editors left out of my segment on *The Doctors* but I have also tried stem cell treatments. I've tried having someone chant over me while I was sitting in a teepee, doing breathwork and meditation while another person dripped oil over me. None of it made a measurable difference in my experience of pain.

But what makes CRPS the hardest thing I've gone through isn't necessarily the debilitating physical pain. No, being diagnosed and told I was going to be in that pain for the rest of my life—that there is no cure for it—was worse. It was devastating to know I would continue to wake up every day like Bill Murray in *Groundhog Day*. No matter what I did to change things, I would still get out of bed and be in pain.

I don't know if a person ever truly gets used to that. The fire of it; the ceaselessness. It's possible to adapt; I know that because that's what I've done. I've found ways of getting around and shifting my mindset so I don't fall into a depression.

That doesn't change the fact that pain is pain and it demands to be heard. Stuff it down, cover it up all you want. It will always rise to the surface.

I say that as someone who has always had a high pain tolerance. That's the gift of being an athlete, a dancer with bloodied feet inside her pointe shoes who keeps pirouetting because she lives and breathes a single mantra: *the show must go on.* But that was before CRPS. When you wake up every day and to the feeling of a million rubber bands twisted around your foot in a vice grip and battery acid burning through your veins all the way up your back—and you know it will never end—well. Sometimes that wears on a person.

I like to be a puppy upper, not a doggie downer. I choose to not complain and I keep my pain to myself because I don't want anyone else to feel sorry for me and because it's even worse when I see how my pain causes the people I love to suffer when they see me in such a state.

But my husband and daughters know me well enough that they can see it in my eyes. I don't have to say anything at all. I can be standing in Target or in line at the post office, and Ruby will say, "Mom, why don't you just go sit down right over there?"

"No, baby," I'll say. "I'm okay."

"Well, Mom, how about this? Stand on one leg, like this." And she'll demonstrate. (My girl. She's got her mama's persistence.)

Ruby is very empathetic. Johnny, he worries. He'll redirect me from driving myself to an event to taking an Uber. "I don't want you driving," he'll say. "Your pain is always intensified at night."

He's right, of course, so I'll take an Uber. But we all know Ubers add up. In fact, my life costs more because of the CRPS diagnosis. I regularly spend more money on medication, supplements, rehab, and the monthly doctors' appointments I have to keep. (That's no fun either. Who wants to go to the doctor once a month?) I also had to buy a self-driving car because CRPS put such a limit on how far I can drive in a regular one.

Just let that sink in for a moment. Driving a regular car puts so much pressure on my foot and intensifies my pain to the point that it becomes unbearable after even short distances. For a number of years, I tried to mitigate that fact by driving with my left foot so I didn't have to constantly hit the gas with my right. But long distance, that gets tricky. And it's a little scary to be hundreds of miles from home and know I might not be able to drive myself back.

Another daily torture is that *I know how to rehab myself from an injury.* I'm an athlete and a trainer. I'd had a whole lifetime of rehabbing my own sprained ankles after running track. Heck, I knew I could help others as a professional trainer *because* I'd rehabbed my own torn meniscus. It was really simple: I got in the gym, I made myself stronger. Not long after, I was able to cancel the surgery doctors said I needed. I always knew that as long as I ate healthy and kept the right mindset, I would get better. I could move on.

But there is no true moving on from CRPS.

I still do all I can to try to heal, and I wake up every day and it's the same. There's no way out. That's a difficult emotional pill to swallow. And although we all have different pain thresholds and different psychological factors that influence how we experience pain—from our emotional states to how easily we hold our attention or become distracted—one of the hardest things has been the cognitive effect.

Listen—I heard the doctors when they told me there was no cure. I understood what they meant when they said I would have this pain for the rest of my life. But that doesn't mean I didn't still have expectations that I would find a way to rehab the pain away, or that I would find a cure. *Screw CRPS*, I thought. *I can beat it.*

And sometimes, that seemed possible. Once, I went in for a spinal block—and just like that, my pain was gone. *Oh my gosh, I did it*, I thought. *I'm cured. This is a miracle.* I was ecstatic.

That afternoon, I was walking through the grocery store on the exquisite high of thinking I was cured. Everything seemed beautiful—the gloss of the apples, the frost clouding the freezer doors—and I was practically weightless, floating down the aisles. But all of a sudden, the pain started coming back. I came crashing back down to reality right along with it.

What goes through a person's mind in a moment like that? I began to grieve the loss of how I felt before as I said goodbye to my old way of doing things. I grieved the person I was before my diagnosis. I felt sadness, discouragement, anger, frustration.

Thankfully, I had given myself the tools to pick myself back up.

Environment, People, and Perception

Our environment has such an impact on how we feel and experience pain. For instance, most people have no idea that I still even have pain—especially when I'm speaking at an event.

That could be because when I'm onstage, it's the only time I feel zero pain.

I honestly don't know if that's because of the adrenaline. I don't know if it's because of the connection I feel with people in the audience when I see joy spark in their eyes because of something I've said. But I do think it is one of the reasons I like to speak so much—not just because of the connection, which I dearly love, but because I feel supported and loved back to the point that I feel no pain.

See, I believe that creating an environment of supportive people—leaders who focus on solutions, instead of victims who focus on suffering—can reduce our perception of pain. When I'm connected like that, my pain recedes. Or, perhaps more accurately, being in that environment and around those people reduces my perception of pain. The reverse is also true. In fact, one of the hardest lessons I've learned is that isolation increases pain. That makes connection the opposite of isolation, and *also* the opposite of addiction.

Let me say that again: connection is the opposite of addiction.

When you're isolated and you feel like no one understands your pain . . . well, that's how I felt when I fell into addiction. I felt like nobody understood my pain, and that made me want to hide it. I didn't want people to see me in pain. I didn't want anyone feeling sorry for me. I slowly started to isolate—a lot like a sick or injured animal following that same primitive instinct. Are they out looking for a mate in those moments or cuddling up with you on the couch? No. They're going to hide. And that's what happened to me. I got disconnected and isolated, and that's when my addiction kicked in full force.

Knowing that is why I've dedicated so much time and space in this book to encourage you to find your people. Find that true support system that will hunt you down when you try to hide. Find those people who will remind you who you are, bring you back into connection, and help you change your perception of pain.

Movement over Addiction

When people are in pain, it's natural to not want to move. The desire to lay on the couch abounds. That's understandable, but I think it's where a lot of people get into trouble. Lying around can easily turn into pills, alcohol, porn, overeating—whatever vice a person's tendency to addiction is oriented toward is what inactivity can open the door to.

I was lucky to learn at an early age that moving your body moves your mood. I could dance or run, and although I was in pain from the sexual abuse I was experiencing, I knew every time I ran track or danced and moved my body, I would feel better. I could diminish my pain.

Back in those days, when I was so young, I didn't know what an endorphin was. I didn't know what a neurotransmitter was. But these are our bodies' natural painkillers, and they can really modulate our perception of pain. Variations in our neurotransmitter levels can also affect our bodies' sensitivity to pain. Even on the days when I'm hurting, I still move my body however I can. Some days, that's just sitting down and doing some light curls. Some days it's just walking around the block. Other days, I can do more. While I was working on these pages, I actually had a day where I could do lunges and leg presses. Johnny saw me doing them and said, "Oh my gosh, Amberly, doesn't that hurt? Your leg is actually bowing out."

"Yeah, it hurts a little," I admitted, "but I know that this is going to make me stronger and it's going to make me feel better."

And it did.

The thing is, moving my body makes everything feel better. I can be having a hard day—whether it's stress from carrying the weight of my deadlines, or stress caused by actual physical pain, or even stress that *causes* actual physical pain—and as soon as I get to the gym and start doing exercises, even when I don't feel like it, I feel better immediately. I might feel like I want to stay home and binge Netflix, but getting to the gym will make me feel better mentally, physically, and even spiritually (depending on what I'm listening to through my headphones).

Reflection: Dispelling Common Myths About Healing

Myth 1: Some Kinds of Pain Trump Other Kinds of Pain

No—pain is pain. It doesn't matter how big or how little.

One day I was at home, after I'd had about 30 surgeries on my leg, and I was hobbling around on crutches. That day, I'd decided to bake a pecan pie. I was upstairs when I realized it was time for that pie to come out of the oven.

I knew the right way to go down the stairs on crutches, but I was in a hurry to get to that pie. *I can just get there faster if I just use my crutches and don't hang onto the rail with one arm. I'll just book it down the stairs.*

Well, halfway down one crutch got stuck in the carpet, and I went flying. I fell face first into the floor, but not before I caught myself with my hands. My left arm snapped on impact, and my whole arm just hung at my side. I will never forget the feeling of the floor rushing up at me—to this day, it's why I still cling to the rail anytime I take the stairs.

My oldest daughter, Savanna, had heard everything. She came running down the stairs behind me. "Holy *shit*, Mom," she said—and she never cusses. "Your arm is broken."

"It's okay."

"No, it's not okay. Your arm is *broken*."

I wasn't even crying at that point. But I needed to go to the hospital, that much was clear, and I couldn't drive myself—also clear. So I called Johnny.

"Could you come home?" I asked. "I think I need to go to the hospital. You can just drop me off at the ER."

"What's wrong?"

"Oh, just get home. I'm okay—I just need you to get me to the ER."

When Johnny got home, I hid my broken arm behind my back.

"You don't want to look at this," I warned. But he insisted, so I pulled my arm back around and let him see. My wrist flopped over to the side.

And off to the hospital we went.

A few hours later, the ER doctors had me in a temporary cast and told me I needed surgery. We went home and had some of my pecan pie. It turned out to be a good one—maybe not worth the broken arm, but a good pie all the same.

The next day, I hobbled into my orthopedic surgeon's office, my arm purple all the way up to my shoulder in that temporary cast, in blinding pain from bones that were set but still broken. A guy in the waiting room turned to me and said, "Oh man, what happened to you?"

"I was in a motorcycle accident."

"Oh yeah," he nodded. "I had a motorcycle accident once. I broke my pinky—and that was *it* for me."

There I was, an absolute mess, and I wouldn't quit going—and this guy's pain threshold was a broken pinky? I still get a good laugh out of that. But, hilarious or not, that broken pinky was his real threshold for pain—bad enough to get him to leave motorcycle riding in his rearview. It's like I said. Pain is pain.

What's painful to a person depends on the person. For some, the pain of a breakup is the worst kind they feel; others get over it faster. Some people see what's happening in the world politically, and that is the worst pain they experience. Me, I'm not into politics, but I'll never forget going to dinner with a friend of mine who was in tears over politics. I couldn't understand it, but I could see the pain she was experiencing was real.

Physical pain is the worst thing many of us experience. Even then, there are different thresholds of tolerance. I split my head open and needed nine stitches once. When the ER doctor came around to numb me so he could put the stitches in,

I said, "Can we just super glue this together?" Apparently that wasn't going to work, so I said, "You don't have to numb me. Just stitch me up." He looked at me like I was crazy (he didn't know I have CRPS), but I didn't even flinch. I deal with excruciating nerve pain every day. CRPS is ranked highest on the pain scale, even worse than an amputation. So—a busted head? To me, that was nothing.

When I was still part of that support group that turned on me, members in the group would often try to out-pain each other. I never understood that. I have an equally difficult time understanding when people say something to me like, "My pain is nothing like yours, and I feel like I shouldn't tell you about what's hurting me because you deal with so much pain."

Again, pain isn't a contest. Pain is pain and we just have to acknowledge it and see what we can do—what solutions we can find—to keep moving forward.

Myth 2: Healing Is Linear

Before I was diagnosed with CRPS, I honestly thought healing was linear. I thought I would get stronger, and then I'd be fine. I had to understand that whether the pain was physical, emotional, or psychological, it doesn't follow a straightforward or predictable path. It involves ups and downs. Progress and setbacks. And there are so many reasons why.

Even when we heal from a trauma, we will always carry symptoms of what came before.

My sexual abuse began when I was eight years old, and I have done a lot to heal from that trauma. For a long time, in fact, I considered it healed. But recently Rachel Lambert, the founder of Braincode Centers, did a mapping of my bran. She looked at my brain scans and was able to see that I'd had trauma—and, within an astonishingly accurate window, what age I was when it occurred.

The clinic staff explained to me that our brains act like hard drives—they store everything we've ever been through. Even if you've done talk therapy or read books or listened to podcasts and think you've dealt with your trauma, the record of it is preserved in your brain.

Rachel could see the spot on my brain that was lit up like red neon in the images and proceeded with the brain mapping. And it was wild—for a moment, I was convinced that she was a psychic. She didn't know me, and yet there she was, telling me exactly how I operate and what had happened to me through my life.

For me, that explains why trauma survivors can still experience triggering events even when they've done the necessary work and feel healed. Me, I might have done the work to deal with my abuse, but the pain of it can still be triggered. That actually happened not long ago: I was in the bedroom, and Johnny came in, and the sound of the doorknob took me right back to the time when I was a little girl, hearing the doorknob to my room when my stepdad was about to come in. I'm lucky that Johnny is so supportive because I freaked out. And I was angry—not at my husband, but because I thought, *No. I healed this trauma*.

The neurofeedback I received during my brain mapping helped me realize that simply isn't the case. So many factors play into the process of recovery and healing, and triggering events like stress, environmental changes, and physical activity all play a role in what often feels like a rollercoaster. Up and down, up and down, up and down. But the good news is, there are ways to continue to feel better and to optimize our brains. There are different tools we can use to recognize our triggers and help ourselves through those triggering events.

And you know something? That makes me appreciate the moments when I feel good even more. I've learned to accept that what's up must go down, and what's down will actually go back up—as long as we choose to.

We can choose to get back up by creating good habits and leaning into them. When I was diagnosed with CRPS, I had to change everything about what I ate. As an athlete, I'd always been a healthy eater, but because of the physical CRPS pain I had to cut out any inflammatory foods, like sugar and alcohol, from my diet. Otherwise, I'll wake up in even more pain the next day. But making lasting changes to my habits and behaviors helped.

It also involved trial and error. Take it from me—as you learn what works for you and what makes your life better, you will experience periods of success and relapse. That's just life. Still, you have to have the courage to *try*. You have to be willing to fail and pick yourself up by trying something new. And then, when you begin to find what works, you have to be incredibly diligent and persistent and dedicated to making lasting change. And give yourself grace when you slip up—because you will slip up. I do, all the time.

I'm coming to the end of a season of not feeling great, and just recently I am starting to feel better. My body is beginning to recover and I'm finally feeling more like myself. But it has taken months of needing to crash on the couch between Zoom meetings, taking planned days off after speaking events, and even losing muscle because I needed so much rest to get me there. I've gotten pretty good at juggling it all, but if I've learned anything, it's that we all have to be our own advocates. We have to listen to our bodies and our intuitions and give ourselves grace through the low times.

Healing isn't linear, but there's beauty and joy in that. It means that when we feel low, we can know we'll eventually feel better again. *I've gotten better before*, I'll tell myself. *I'll get better again.*

Take comfort in that, and believe in your ability to heal.

Myth 3: Once You've Found Joy, You're Always Joyful; Once You've Found Healing, You're Always Healed

This simply isn't the way things work. It oversimplifies the complex and dynamic nature of human emotion and the healing process.

Fluctuating emotions are a normal part of life. Relationships shift, following the ebb and flow of our lives. And our circumstances are always going to change. Take our finances, for instance. I hear from a lot of my clients—many of whom are highly successful in the real estate industry—that they are afraid that sky-high interest rates and a volatile election year will threaten their ability to keep their own home. Changes are constant, and constantly unexpected. Nobody thought the entire world would shut down when COVID happened, but that didn't stop it from happening.

When change happens we might not feel very joyful, but the fact is we can build on the joy we do have in our lives. It's there inside us—we just have to tap into it. Experiencing sadness and anger and all the other parts of the human experience just makes us appreciate that joy even more. Certain changes or triggers might bring back difficult feelings, but our overall goal and trend can be toward healing.

And the truth is, we are always changing. Hopefully that's because we're always growing, but it's also because we have constantly evolving needs and desires. When I was little, for instance, I loved fishing. I'd go all by myself—I'd get out of school, grab my pole, and away I'd go because it filled me with so much joy. Now, baiting a hook with a worm isn't such a magical experience for me. But Ruby loves it the way I used to, and it brings me joy to see the way fishing lights her up inside.

Understanding that joy and healing are not permanent states will help you set realistic expectations. It will also encourage you to have ongoing self-care and do persistent emotional work. Personally, I think it enables you to give yourself some grace and compassion, and to give even more compassion to others.

I like to say change is possible and hope is available, but the choice to seize them is yours. You have to decide that you want to move forward and be the victor of your life. Nobody can make that choice for you. Nobody was going to walk for me back when I was completely bedridden. I had to learn to walk myself.

So many people today, even my clients, just want to wait for opportunities to happen. But you can't do that. You have to create opportunities. You can't just sit around waiting to be healed. You've got to actively participate in your own healing.

Oprah has said, "I know for sure what we dwell on is who we become." I would only add that we have to attempt to find the good that can exist, even inside the dark times, and we will find what we're looking for. When you hunt for good, more good things come into your life. Maybe you could start dwelling on the good with the same prayer I recite when I'm feeling uneasy. It's most commonly associated with St. Francis of Assisi, and it goes like this: "Lord, make me a channel for thy peace. That where there is hatred, I may bring love. That where there is wrong, I may bring the spirit of forgiveness. And that where there is discord, I may bring harmony. That where there is error, I may bring truth."

Actionable Steps

Unleash your superpower with my PACER method. This methodology is the life-changing tool that strengthens your resilience so you can rise up, despite any adversity, and persevere through any of life's challenges. Reflect on the biggest challenge you're facing right now. Walk through the PACER method and write down all the things you can do to be more resilient.

Perspective. You have the power and the choice to transform your life with a simple shift in your perspective. It's not necessarily what's happening in our world but how we view it. The quickest way to shift your perspective is to count your blessings, get grateful, focus on the positive, or hunt for the good. Gratitude is alchemy. It turns what we don't have into what we do have and what we can't do into what we can do.

Acceptance. True acceptance is the first step to freedom and becoming the best version of yourself. It's recognizing that you are ready to make changes necessary to have the best life possible and thrive. It is the beginning of starting where you are, using what you have, and doing what you can to evolve. It's getting brutally honest with yourself.

Community. You are never alone. Together, we are unstoppable. Humans are hardwired for connection. We need it to survive and thrive. Now more than ever, safe spaces and building community online can be as important as coming together in person. When we share our story, we build meaningful, deep connections and strengthen our community.

Endurance. Passion + Perseverance = Grit and that is exactly what you need to get through the most challenging times and go after your big goals. When we focus on our why and do things one day at a time and one step at a time, we build our stamina. It takes a willingness to get up every day and jump out of your comfort zone and practice to develop good habits.

Rest. Rest means recovery, refuel, recharge, and reset. It's giving yourself grace and lots of it. It's loving yourself each day and listening to your body and your heart. It's being open-minded to different methods of rest when you're challenged with a never-ending to-do list or are in too much pain to fall asleep.

Key Takeaway

Healing and joy are not about arrival. They're about having the tools to bounce forward.

Conclusion
The Purpose in Pain Opportunity

People ask me all the time if I would take it all back—the motorcycle accident, the sexual abuse, everything I've been through.

The truth is, I wouldn't wish any of it on my worst enemy. But what I've learned is that life is a series of choices we make regardless of what happens in our lives. And through the journey of *my* life, I realized I could have simply . . . given up. I could have been the victim of my circumstances.

Instead, I chose to be the product of my resilience.

Through the many ups and downs in life, I have discovered—in the wake of that resilience—that joy is like a steadfast lighthouse pillar holding firm against the storm. This is the kind of joy that is weathered by many storms. It is a bit worn. Maybe even a little beaten up. And yet, through the crack of lightning and lash of rain, it's unwavering.

One thing I know for sure is that *you* can experience the same relentless, unwavering joy.

See, I'm no different than you. You can make the same choices I have. We can *all* make those choices. We can all choose to notice the gifts of life that are all around us. They really are plentiful.

To see them, all you have to do is look.

Reflection: Nothing Wasted

Pain is inevitable, but suffering is optional. I say God doesn't waste pain because my pain has led me to so many gifts. It has made me closer to God. It has increased my awareness. It has helped me improve as trainer for my client Mary Ellen, who told me I was a better trainer after my accident because I could understand her pain so much better.

If we didn't have pain, we wouldn't develop resilience or grit. Pain and suffering are challenging, but they can also serve as a powerful catalyst for a spiritual awakening and profound personal and spiritual growth.

Pain has made me more empathetic, sensitive, and compassionate to others. It has helped me understand the suffering of others—just like Mary Ellen said. Even something as silly as social media can be an opportunity to be in service to someone else. I always find myself wanting to respond to every single person's comment on every single post I create, because I understand what it feels like to be invisible—to not feel understood, seen, or heard—and I also understand what it can feel like when someone acknowledges *my* comment or responds to me on Instagram. What kind of joy that can spark.

In that way, pain can be a gift. It can be an *opportunity*.

Use it in the right way, and it gives you beautiful things.

I think God doesn't waste pain because my pain pushed me to help others. Every painful experience I've been through has enabled me to connect on a deeper level with others, shift my perspective from pain to purpose and promise, which in turn led to more joy. There's nothing more powerful than being able to connect with someone who understands you, who gives you an opportunity to breathe a sigh of relief and say, "Me, too." Seeing that person make it through their pain to the other side brings so much hope.

I like to say we keep what we give away. Which doesn't make sense, except that it does. I keep my sobriety as long as I'm being of service to others and helping someone else stay sober. I keep my success as an entrepreneur as long as I am a servant leader, being of service to others and their success. And you know something? It's so fulfilling when you can serve others and help facilitate their success. It's a wellspring of joy that leads me to my gratitude practice. I can feel grateful when the pain from complex regional pain syndrome is a 10 because I know it will, at some point, come back down to an 8, or 5, or even a 2.

We heal, and then we go help others. If more of us could do that, the world would be a different place. Pain can motivate us to seek out and find deeper meaning and purpose in life. I shared this pain with the world, and through that experience others have been able to embrace their own scars. I think that makes their world—and mine—a better place to be.

But when I think of the fact that God doesn't waste pain, what I think about most is surrender. Surrendering the idea that I have to do everything on my own. Surrendering the idea that I always, *always* have to grit things out, no matter what. And accepting that when I let go and let God in those situations that were beyond my control, I can simply trust in a power greater than mine.

It takes the pressure off.

It takes the stress off.

I was hired recently to give a keynote in front of thousands of people, and saying I was anxious is an understatement. The pressure was on—not only because I wanted to deliver an impactful message for the event host and all the attendees but also because I wanted to make the speaker bureau that I worked with proud. I had practiced and I had prepared but I only felt better after I remembered it's in God's hands. I took the action and trusted God with the outcome. And you know what? It turned out to be one of the most joyous opportunities I have ever had. And the best part of the entire experience was after the event when I had hundreds of people reaching out to me saying things like, "Your joy was contagious!" and "You give me hope!"

When you do the work and trust God has a plan for you, there will always be opportunities, and the possibilities are endless. It enables you to spark even more joy in your life.

There's a song that says something like "I only call God when I need a favor." In some ways, there's a lot of truth there. Pain can drive us to engage more deeply in spiritual practices like prayer and meditation. Me, I need to stay connected to God, to my higher power, because when I don't it's a little too easy to forget he's there . . . and then things go sideways. But as long as I keep God close, I know I can get through anything.

It all boils down to this: we *can* succumb to our pain.

Or . . .

We can take that pain as the starting point to tap into deeper, lasting, and more abundant joy.

Every single gift I've received through pain has added up to joy beyond measure—the kind capable of shining a light over any sea of hurt, disappointment, or frustration—regardless of the storm or its thrashing.

I want that for you. And I know, beyond any shadow of doubt, that you can have it.

My sincere wish is that you will take my experience and my guidance, even though I'm definitely not a guru, and apply it to your life. I'm in tears right now as I write this part of the book because I am so eternally grateful for the life that I have been given.

Every morning as I roll out of bed the first thing I do is drop to my knees and pray to God that he guides me through the day, lifts the obsession to drink, and keeps me sober one day at a time so that I might be of service to others.

Every single night as I plop into bed, sometimes tired, hurting, or even filled with worry, I say thank you, thank you, thank you, for another day sober. I just keep saying thank you and my mind is at rest and my heart feels at peace.

Now I realize you might not understand the pain that comes along with addiction or an incurable nerve disease, but we all struggle with some sort of pain. Maybe it's physical, maybe it's a break up, maybe it's fear that our bills won't be paid, the love of our life will never show up, or our child is sick. But I know that when we turn it over to our higher power and throughout the day continue to say, "Thy will be done," we are in much less danger of feeling fear, pain, or worry and more inclined for inspiration, creativity, and joy.

There was a time I didn't believe it would be possible to ever feel joy again, ever be happy again, or ever have a life worth living. This might seem extreme, but after all, I was in such a dark place and didn't feel like I could ever climb out of the pit of despair and the debt from so many medical bills. But being willing to do the work on my mind, body and spirit EVERY SINGLE DAY eventually gave me the life of my dreams.

Do I still struggle? Well, yes, but now I have tools to move through that struggle and see the promise and opportunity, and so do you. It's one thing to have a tool box, it's another to actually use those tools. Faith without work is dead. You have to take action. So I hope you take what you need from this book and take action.

Using these tools, my life and my old way of thinking have changed, and yours can, too. I still have no control over some things that happen in my life—none of us do—but with the help of God and the support of others, I choose how I will respond. Today I choose to be happy and spark joy. Today I choose to be a joy sparker in other people's lives and walk throughout the day joy spotting. If I fall off track and when I don't feel joyful, I have these tools to put me back on track.

When I stop living in the problem and living in the answer, the problem goes away. When I concentrate on what needs to be changed in me and my attitude instead of what needs to be changed in the world, I can be free. I can spark joy.

When I am focused on being in acceptance and thinking less about expectations I find serenity.

Not only that, by using these tools, my feelings of despair have been replaced by joy. Feelings of shame replaced by grace, pain into purpose, fear into faith, and all resentment into love.

I used to regret my past but now I find it useful to help someone else who might be struggling. When I get out of myself and go help someone else it not only fills my heart but also helps me not take myself so seriously.

Believe that you have the power to change your life through joy, resilience, and even pain.

Believe that you can use pain in service of someone else.

Believe that you have the power to create the life you've always imagined.

Acknowledgments

I am thankful for all the people who have encouraged me, coached me, and have been by my side to remind me to have joy through the journey of life's ups and downs.

Dr. Mandi Reed, thank you for saving the day with your expertise and advice on writing, insight, and guidance, meeting me at 6 a.m. on so many mornings to assure me that I would get this book written. You are the most amazing writing coach!

Julie Kerr, thank you for being an amazing developmental editor! I was always so nervous to send you my work, and you were so supportive and kind. Thank you for your loving red pen.

Cheryl Segura and Amanda Pyne and the wonderful team at Wiley, thank you for your continued support and guidance with the book. I am in awe of your attentiveness, professionalism, talent, AND kindness. It was always a dream of mine to get my book published with Wiley. I thank you for bringing my dream to life.

Jon Gordon, thank you for planting the seed for this book. I will never forget that one day after we talked and you gave me the title to this book. I wrote it down on a sticky note and it has been on my computer for years! You and Kathryn always spark joy in my life, and I am forever grateful for your friendship, support, and guidance. Also, I cried happy tears when you agreed to write the Foreword for me.

My friends and family who have been by my side and supported my wild and crazy dreams. I love you and I am grateful for you! My sobriety sisters and my sponsor for your love, support, and our gratitude practice together. You keep me grounded, grateful, and help me stay sober. You mean the world to me.

My unstoppable Mastermind ladies! You are always the highlight of my week, and I am blessed to be on this journey with you! We are chosen family, and every single one of you shared and bought my book the minute it was available for presale. I am forever grateful for you, and I love you so much!

Thank you to my mom and dad for being who you are because you made me who I am, and Granny for being my role model.

Johnny, Savanna, and Ruby for being my inspiration, my loves, my life! Thank you for the joy you bring to me! You are my world, my sunshine, my safe haven, my EVERYTHING! And Johnny, I know you were worried about me taking on too much with another book because you care. Thank you for your support and love along the way! I love you with all my heart and you are the best husband in the world, ESPECIALLY for putting up with all my crazy shenanigans.

And finally to God, for walking with me every step of the way, for speaking through me, for being the love that pours through me, and for giving me the strength and courage to pour my heart and soul into this book.

With all the love and gratitude in my heart,
Amberly

About the Author

Amberly Lago is an internationally renowned speaker on grit, resilience, and human connection, captivating audiences at global corporations such as Lululemon, Google, and Athleta. Her TEDx Talk has garnered hundreds of thousands of views, inspiring listeners around the world.

As a highly sought-after thought leader, coach, and best-selling author, Amberly's expertise has been featured in prominent media outlets including *Forbes*, *USA Today* (where she was named one of the nation's top influential speakers), *The Doctors*, Hallmark, and *The TODAY Show*.

Her podcast, *The Amberly Lago Show*, ranks in the top 1% globally, as recognized by Apple, where she shares impactful insights with leading experts and influencers.

Throughout her career, Amberly has empowered thousands of clients to overcome personal and professional challenges, guiding them toward achieving unstoppable success.

Amberly's own story of resilience is equally remarkable. After a devastating motorcycle accident and 34 surgeries to save her leg, she emerged stronger by developing her signature PACER method—a powerful framework that teaches how authentic connections foster resilience, joy, and lasting success. More detail is available on website at amberlylago.com.

Index